EMERGENCE

Hidden Narratives from Neurodivergent Social Workers

Edited by
Kelly Bentley-Simon & Siobhan Maclean

Published by
Kirwin Maclean Associates
4 Mesnes Green, Lichfield
Staffordshire
WS14 9AB

enquiries@kirwinmaclean.com
www.kirwinmaclean.com
01543 417800

First published in 2023
Kirwin Maclean Associates
4 Mesnes Green,
Lichfield Staffordshire
WS14 9AB

Graphic design by Tora Kelly
Front Cover artwork by Clair Girvan
Back Cover artwork by David Grimm
Inside photography by Nat Photography Northern Ireland
Printed and bound in Great Britain by 4edge, Essex

Everyone involved in the process and product of this anthology is neurodivergent. All the contributors and both editors, the designer, typesetter and photographer are all neurodivergent.

ISBN 9781912130764
eBook 9781912130979

A catalogue record for this book will be available from The British Library.

Neurodiversity may be every bit as crucial for the human race as biodiversity is for life in general. Who can say what form of wiring will be best at any given moment?

- Harvey Blume. The Atlantic 1998

We have tied our self-worth to their statements and at some point, we must begin the slow and arduous process of breaking free and seeing that we are more than they said we were.

- Kaiya Stone

Contents

About the Editors

- *Kelly Bentley-Simon*

Kelly Bentley-Simon is a social worker, currently working within the area of child and adolescent mental health. She qualified in as a social worker in 2022 and has worked in many related areas before this, from youth and community work, family support, safeguarding and education.

Kelly's current work involves working in a multidisciplinary team, carrying out ADHD and Autism assessments with children and young people aged 18 and younger, followed by formal diagnoses and communicating these to the family. Doing this work in a team with a large number of neurodivergent workers has helped Kelly to understand more about herself and how her brain works, learning more about neurodivergence every day.

Kelly was diagnosed with the specific learning difference – Dyscalculia, sometime around 2011, and later on with Attention Deficit Hyperactivity Disorder (ADHD) in 2021. As a neurodivergent social worker, Kelly recognises that learning is often not a linear path, and at times a love of learning is not enough. Some people simply need more time to get where they need to be.

In 2020, Kelly and Siobhan worked together with others, to plan and deliver a program of support to social workers and students who were unable to continue their social work studies due to the pandemic, with Kelly leading on a webinar exploring neurodivergence and social work. Building on the success of this session, the idea for this anthology was born.

Kelly hopes that this anthology of narratives from neurodivergent social workers will help to improve knowledge and understanding of neurodivergence, highlighting some of the challenges that being neurodivergent brings, balanced with the strengths that being neurodivergent brings to the profession.

Twitter @Kelly_BFD

- *Siobhan Maclean*

Siobhan Maclean has been a social worker for 33 years and a practice educator for 29 years. Siobhan works independently providing training and consultancy services to social work employers and Universities. She has a particular passion for supporting students and practitioners in the areas of theory and practice and reflective practice.

In 2013 Siobhan had a stroke. This impacted on her work and her understanding of social work in many ways, as experiencing services often does. Since that time, she has not been a direct case holder, although she still supports other social workers in discussing their work directly. She also still works as an off-site practice educator.

Siobhan is committed to ensuring that there is a platform for the voices of people with varied experiences of social work and spends time supporting social workers and people with lived experience to write for publication.

In 2021 along with Wayne Reid, Siobhan edited Outlanders: Hidden Narratives from Social Workers of Colour. In 2022 along with Mary Carter, Siobhan edited Insiders Outsiders: Hidden Narratives of Care Experienced Social Workers. This third anthology feels particularly important to Siobhan as she is a neurodivergent social worker herself.

Twitter @SiobhanMaclean

Website www.siobhanmaclean.co.uk

I am different, not less.

- Temple Grandin

PREFACE

Why the title: What do we mean by EMERGENCE?

- *Siobhan Maclean and Kelly Bentley-Simon*

When we met together for the first time to look at the submissions for the book, we started to think about a title for the collection. We wanted the title to be in keeping with the first two anthologies of social work narratives and started to play around with words around diverging. Reflecting back on that 'word play' if anyone else had been there, it would probably have been an excellent observation of neurodivergent thinking. Two neurodivergent people throwing in ideas of words might have looked chaotic, but isn't that what creativity looks like sometimes? In this short explanation we hope to share with you the process and what the title word means to us.

We began that weekend by looking at what we saw as 'emerging' themes and had a light bulb moment when emerging rather than diverging spoke to us as a word. The Oxford English Dictionary definition of 'emerge' is "*to move out of or away from something and become possible to see.*" Do a google search on definitions of emergence and you will find phrases like "*the process of becoming visible after being concealed.*" Of course, we want this anthology to enable visibility, and this linked into one of the emerging themes around invisibility and neurodivergence being concealed.

At this point, one of the emerging themes we had noted was around water, there was a clear sense that people were drowning or being submerged. David Grimm had submitted his artwork 'Drowning in Plain Sight' and we saw the image as a person emerging from the water. Most of the artwork that Clair Girvan submitted has links with the sea. Katie Küken shares her experiences of "*drowning in treacle when faced with tasks I can't picture or predict."* Kulchuma Begum powerfully describes her diagnosis as *"my lifejacket that helped keep me afloat even in the stormiest of seas."* We were very excited to receive a submission from Hong Kong and interested that in this too, Yulin Cheng included references to water explaining that the *"months ahead are going to be an intense roller coaster ride on turbulent waters."* The submissions at that point gave us a real sense that our contributors felt 'at sea' and we hoped that being able to 'emerge' from this might speak to our authors and readers alike. We hope that when reading this collection people will feel supported to emerge. In the striking poem 'Who am I?' Karen Gilbank says *"No longer am I drowned"* we hope that people may feel this way when they work through the contributions in this anthology.

When we selected the word 'emergence' and started to think about it in more detail it struck us that with an exchange of the final letter, the word becomes 'emergency.' Supporting our neurodivergent colleagues has now reached a level of emergency. Social workers are exhausted and exiting the profession at a rapid pace. Many of those workers are neurodivergent and have not been given the support they need. Social work is facing a real emergency and now is the time for the strengths of all social workers to emerge.

Our hope for this anthology is that it can be read and used by different sectors of the profession. Some people may read this book cover to cover, and some may select specific sections they feel are useful. For social work students we would recommend "You Belong Here" by Jenni Guthrie as a useful starting point. For an exploration of 'hidden' neurodivergence we would recommend the reflections from Caroline Aldridge and Maximillian Hawker. For those considering the possibility that they might be neurodivergent, and what this might mean, we would recommend the reflections from Sandy Symonds and Chris Norman. Wherever you start, we know that every single piece in the anthology is honest, personal and very much needed.

Creating Connections Around the 'Rule of Three'

- *Siobhan Maclean*

This is the third anthology of social worker's narratives that I have edited. The first anthology was 'Outlanders: Hidden Narratives from Social Workers of Colour' and the second 'Insiders Outsiders: Hidden Narratives of Care Experienced Social Workers.' In some ways I have found this anthology much more complex to bring together than the previous ones, I have reflected on why this might be and have concluded that there are a range of reasons (aren't there always a range of reasons for everything?) Firstly, contributions have come in many different formats - via many different channels, neurodivergent people are often more creative but for an editor this can be extra challenging. This is the first anthology which I have contributed to as an author, and I wonder whether this has made it more complex. I have also experienced a number of changes in my own life as the anthology has been coming together. Complexity, challenge and change are all connected: Change often creates challenges, challenges can create change, change and challenge *are* complex. Bringing this anthology together was challenging and complex but we hope it will create change.

Recognising the complexity, challenge and change in the process of compiling the anthology reminded me of the 'rule of three' referred to by Aristotle, the Ancient Greek philosopher in his book 'Rhetoric: dramatic unity of time, place and action'. The basis of the rule is that when things are presented in threes the message is clearer. Neurodivergent people are often more able to see or create connections, certainly this is something that I have noticed in myself since I became neurodivergent. Once I thought of the rule of three, I saw so many connections around 'threes' within the anthology.

As we send this manuscript to print it is three years since Covid19 first impacted in the UK. All the anthologies have been published since the first Covid lockdowns and there have been reflections on this in all three anthologies. In this text, many of the reflections make reference to Covid and the impact that it has had on peoples' lives and experiences. Most interestingly, it is clear from reading the reflections that a number of people started to question their own neurotype during the Covid lockdowns, with a number of people receiving a diagnosis during this time. Covid has had a significant impact on social work and the way it is delivered, with social workers now often working in a 'hybrid' or 'blended' way. It has become clearer to me reading this anthology that there are specific issues around neurodiversity and the changes that Covid have bought about in social work, and I feel that this needs more consideration at higher management level.

In the training I deliver around social work theory and reflective practice I almost always refer to Temple Grandin's work on three different thinking styles. There has long been an idea that some people think in words and others think in pictures. An autistic woman, Temple Grandin (2006) claimed that people think in one of three main ways: Verbal thinkers tend to think in words, they tend to adopt logical thinking styles and find verbal communication easy. Visual thinkers tend to think in pictures and images, people who are visual thinkers often form memories around images rather than words. Visual thinkers generally have good observation skills. Mathematical / musical thinkers tend to think in patterns, they often see relationships between things as patterns. This book, more than any other I have ever worked on draws together all three thinking styles. We had a number of art submissions, such that we have created an artwork section which none of the other anthologies include. The reflections also draw on visual thinking a great deal with analogies throughout. The patterns that authors discuss also demonstrate mathematical / musical thinking.

As the collection of submissions came together, we had three sections – reflections, poetry and artwork. However, when Kelly and I looked at this we decided that we wanted to add a fourth section of 'Advice'. We speculated that people may look to this book to provide advice and whilst many of the reflections contain advice for neurodivergent practitioners we thought a separate section on advice would be helpful. Three of our authors provided some specific advice and Kelly and I worked together to pull out the advice from the collection adding a little of our own advice.

When looking at the trilogy of narratives together, I have noted three specific themes that emerge in each anthology connecting them together. The first of these connecting themes is the thread of invisibility and silence. In the previous narratives, social workers of colour and care experienced social workers shared experiences of being unseen and unheard. In this collection there are many references to being invisibilised and silenced. Mark Stockley-Haycock tells us of his experiences in school "*I struggled on in silence, ashamed and afraid to speak up about anything*" a theme that is reflected in many of the contributions. In her poem about the daily Russian Roulette of being a neurodivergent social worker, Hannah illustrates the way that sometimes silence is a result of fear or shame "*So, I've often stayed quiet, in fear of making errors.*" The subtitle to all three of the anthologies refers to "hidden narratives" and this comes through in this collection perhaps more than in any of the other anthologies. Caroline Aldridge refers to her "*hidden disability*", one of Clair Girvan's pieces of art is titled the 'Hidden Rainbow' and Maximillian Hawker tells us that "*Most of the time, OCD is the very definition of a hidden illness.*" I was particularly struck by Deb recounting her experiences of being "*that child who would be hidden away when school inspectors arrived.*" I wonder if the extensive experiences of being hidden is what makes many of the authors here astute to what may be invisible to others, indeed in her author page, Belle Penhaligon explains that one of her strengths is "*seeing the unseen.*" I hope that this collection of hidden narratives helps people to feel more seen and more heard, something which is particularly important on a number of levels. Florence Smith asserts the importance of representation in her reflection explaining that "*I wish I had explicitly seen another neurodivergent social worker and had the opportunity to listen to their journey.*"

In the prefaces to the previous anthologies, I have shared something of my learning about language from reading the collections. Once again, the use of language has been a key learning point for me in the process of compiling this book. The word language actually appears many times in the anthology, with authors sharing their struggles with language as a result of their neurodivergence, in fact I lost my ability to use or read language when I had my stroke. A word that I have always avoided is suffered. In my professional life I had always challenged the use of the word suffered as I felt it held judgment, and when I had a stroke, I hated hearing "suffered a stroke." However, the word suffer appears in Maximillian Hawker's powerful reflection seven times and Hannah shares that she has "*suffered with OCD since I was around ten years old, and ADHD as long as I can remember.*" Diana Katoto tells us that "*I was a black child in an educational system that allowed me to slip through the net. I look back on my experience and realise that if I was provided with support and strategies earlier, I wouldn't have had to suffer as much.*" It is clear in reading this anthology that authors have suffered, and still suffer. On reflection I have learnt that the word 'suffer' can be very powerful in demonstrating what is happening for people and if a person chooses to use that word, then I will use that in my conversations with them to ensure that they feel their experiences are heard and their 'suffering' is validated. Language is constantly changing, and of course of our understanding of language will change too. I have learnt a great deal from Kelly about the use of language and I know that she has recently been thinking about the deficit-based language often used in assessments. As a result of reading the submissions as this anthology has been building, I have found myself wondering about the language of diagnosis and whether this is deficit or strengths based and this has certainly challenged my own thinking and encouraged me to think more deeply about language. As you read this anthology, I would encourage you to think about your own use of language.

Love, kindness and belonging have been themes in each of the three anthologies. I have often wondered if I have seen these themes because I have been looking for them. In my own work I talk of love and kindness often, but even if I wasn't looking for it, the word 'love' appears in this book 57 times. The authors tell us that they love to learn and love to create, but most of all many of the contributors tell us that they love their work. The number of times that you will read in this anthology *"I love social work"* is uplifting. I have never seen this expressed so consistently and strongly in any book about social work.

In terms of kindness many of the reflections remind us of the power of kindness. The vital importance of self-kindness really comes through in this anthology. Many of the authors share with us their own inner critic and explore the vital importance of working on being kind to ourselves. Deb Solomon shares *"What I have noticed is that I am kinder to myself post diagnosis."* On the contrary I feel that my own self kindness has been impacted by becoming neurodivergent, maybe I have felt a pressure to prove that I can "work" and so I have worked harder and harder leaving myself little time to relax. I have resolved to concentrate more on getting a work life balance and to be kinder to myself. Anonymous tells us *"I am trying to afford myself the kindness that I have always tried to offer others"* and I am going to join them in this.

The title of Jenni Guthrie's reflection tells us *"You Belong Here."* I have noticed that a number of the reflections talk of belonging in relation to receiving a diagnosis, Rose Matthews says *"Finding out that I am autistic has given me a renewed sense of belonging and purpose"* and Karen Gilbank shares *"at the age of 43 I was diagnosed with ADHD and Autism – I finally felt like I belonged and could be my true self, quirks, and all.*" Thinking about this, I found Sandy Symonds reflection very helpful "*Having a formal diagnosis can also feel supportive, the opportunity to connect with other neurodiverse individuals, perhaps leading to a sense of belonging. The downside to focusing so much on individual diagnoses and "pigeon holing" a group of people as neurodiverse, can be to take away from their individual uniqueness.*" It is vital that a sense of belonging should not impact on our recognition of uniqueness. Maya Angelou refers to diversity making a rich tapestry. I recall Wayne Reid referring to the first collection of narratives from social workers of colour as providing a rich tapestry. Perhaps it is diversity that provides a golden thread through all three anthologies.

During the time that we were compiling this anthology I moved house, in fact I moved to a new country and culture. I lived in my previous community for over 30 years, and I have lived where I am now for just eighteen months and yet I have a sense of belonging here that I never had in my previous place. As I have thought about the theme of belonging in this anthology, I have reflected on why that might be. Why do I feel such a sense of connection and belonging in this new area? There are of course a number of reasons which include the strong sense of collective reflection through storytelling and songs which create a shared culture that I have been warmly welcomed into. My curiosity and cultural humility has been valued and people have been happy to share their experiences and wisdom with me. Maybe the experiences that people have had of Covid and the sense that avoiding isolation is important has also had an impact. Time and place have come together well for me and that sense of belonging has been really positive and uplifting. I have always had a sense of belonging to the profession of social work and that has also been positive and uplifting for me during the thirty-seven years since I started my social work course. I am sad that so many social workers don't necessarily have that sense of belonging to the profession and I hope that the stories and wisdom contained in this book might help neurodivergent social workers and aspiring social workers feel that sense of belonging. I would encourage you to use what is contained in this book as an opportunity for shared reflection, share the contents with your colleagues as this may start some important conversations.

Perhaps the key thing that connects all three anthologies is the oppression that the practitioners have faced not only in their wider life, but within the profession itself. What does that tell us about that golden thread of diversity? Social work is a profession built on social justice and a commitment to anti-oppressive practice. Prospera Tedam's excellent 4D2P model (Tedam 2021) helps us to understand the difference between being non-oppressive and anti-oppressive, with the key being whether we disrupt the oppression that people face. It is clear in this anthology that the profession is not welcoming or even non-oppressive towards neurodivergent practitioners. We must look at what we can do to disrupt the negative experiences of all neurodivergent people. The authors in this anthology are trailblazing disrupters. Many were described in their childhood as disruptive as though this was a bad thing. Good social work is all about disruption.

I want to conclude where I started with Aristotle's rule of three outlined in his book 'Rhetoric: dramatic unity of time, place and action.' Let's try to use that in our future practice – creating a dramatic unity of time, place and action to bring about positive change.

References

Tedam, P. (2021) Anti-Oppressive Social Work Practice. (London) Sage Learning Matters.

Grandin, T. (2006) *Thinking in Pictures: and other reports from my life with autism*. Expanded Edition. (New York) Doubleday Publishing.

Challenges, Connections and Communities

- Kelly Bentley-Simon

Siobhan and I started working together in 2020 during the Covid19 pandemic. A period of time characterised by difficult circumstances. The ability to connect with others taken away, but with a desire to reach out and 'be' with others, thus intentionally or not, creating connections and supporting ourselves.

Both of us in very different but equally challenging situations.

These connections took the form of a group of social work students, plus Siobhan, planning and delivering a series of online webinars to support social workers and students in a time of uncertainty while universities, workplaces and public buildings were closed. No one knew how long these webinars would last, or what the long-term plan was, but as time went on and my confidence grew, I expressed the idea of a webinar exploring neurodiversity and how we as a profession might learn about and support neurodivergent social workers and students. Looking back, I'm not sure whether this was an idea, a want, or a need; it was possibly all three. Whatever it was, Siobhan provided a platform, space, and support.

Building on the webinar, the idea for this anthology was born, a comment I made about wishing there was a book on the topic was picked up Siobhan and returned to me many months later, I can't remember the exact wording, but it was something along the lines of, "*Remember when you said we should write a book about neurodivergence and social work? Let's do it.*" At the time, I was surprised that I had made the comment aloud outside of my own thoughts, but it I couldn't deny that it *did* sound like something I would say. What surprised more, was that Siobhan remembered me saying it, agreed there was a gap, and wanted to be involved.

In the early stages of the project, I hoped that this anthology of narratives from neurodivergent social workers and students would help to improve knowledge and understanding of neurodivergence. Highlighting some of the challenges that being neurodivergent brings, balanced with the strengths that neurodivergent social workers bring to the profession. However, my learning from this project has been so much more than I ever thought it might.

I'm not sure how other people would describe me, but I think 'Jack of all trades' might be most peoples' view, and I wouldn't necessarily disagree with this. I can turn my hand to most things and do a fairly good job. I wouldn't say I necessarily excel at anything in particular, the majority of my school reports described me as "a good all-rounder", and I think this is fairly accurate. The reason I say this, is not to downplay my abilities or appear humble, but because I have never been involved in any kind of editing before, therefore, I had no view on whether this was something I could do, or not.

However, what I found is that editing a book is much more difficult than I thought it would be, and this is with someone as experienced as Siobhan as my co-editor. In early conversations, Siobhan revealed that this is possibly one of the most difficult books that she has edited. This didn't make the process easier, but helped provide perspective, it *was* difficult, I wasn't the only one struggling, but we *could* do it!

After the first of many final deadlines for call outs for submissions, Siobhan and I met in person to review what had been sent in so far. Our process was simple, we both had copies of each submission, we would read them independently, make notes then meet to discuss our thoughts. For me, this was a simple process that worked well. During this process, my notes showed a number of strong themes, most that I expected, but some that I did not.

In those early sessions, the most common first theme was that of helplessness and hopelessness, of drowning; the struggles of being neurodivergent in a neurotypical world that just isn't designed for you. The second, was a theme of self-acceptance; the uphill realisation of being different, not less, and reconciling with this. The final theme was that of justification. The desperation of "*...yes I have this difficulty, but I'm also good at some stuff too, watch how well I can juggle!*"

As the editing process went on, and we reviewed the next batch of submissions, I saw the themes begin to change. Although I can't be certain whether it was the content of the submissions or my perspective that changed. Whatever the reason, during this time I began to see themes of sadness but also hope. The symbolism of drowning while also wanting to fade into the background was still there, but it was coupled with a raw, deep sadness at 'what could have been'. Vicky Butterfield describes the feelings of shame experienced from a lifetime of being told she is 'too much', "*It is hard to express the hurt which occurs when you are measured by the wrong stick*". Vicky's sadness for the childhood version of herself is echoed in Zebra, as Sandy Symonds explores '*the what if's?*' In fact, we have a whole piece entitled "What If?", where Maximillian Hawker provides much needed education and insight into what life is like for him with OCD, a very different take on the theme of 'what if?' but equally as valued and needed. As Maximillian tells us, what is needed isn't shame, condemnation, or sympathy, but understanding; echoing the theme of harmful societal messages which inevitably lead to the internalisation of these harmful views, tarnishing our view of ourselves.

As we draw this project to a close, having read and reread all of the contributions, I am struck by the themes that I now see within the body of work as a whole. Taking a physical and metaphorical step back with Siobhan to view each submission and where it might be best placed within the book has enabled me to see each reflection, poem and piece of artwork as an 'anthology', a whole complete piece of work. Separate pieces by individual people that exist on their own but are also a part of something that is bigger than the sum of its parts.

Having read this anthology as a whole, I am left with thoughts and feelings of positivity, pride and hope. I have been urged to remember that 'I belong here' by Jenni Guthrie, in fact, we have been gently reminded of the impact, the need for, and the result of a lack of belonging by Jenni Guthrie, Karen Gilbank, Sandy Symonds and Rose Matthews. For me, the opposite of 'not belonging' is community. Not belonging *to* a community but *being* a community. In the same way that peace is more than the absence of war, community is a conscious, deliberate act, it is a disruption. Florence Smith reminds us of the importance of psychological safety and how this secure foundation is instrumental in allowing a person to be themself, Siobhan tells us that we can be psychologically safe on our own, but true psychological safety is found with others. The importance of finding a community runs through this whole anthology, again, reinforced by Siobhan in her reflection on the concept of Ubuntu "*We become people through our connections with other people*".

As my thoughts on this project draw to a close, I am once again brought back to the initial themes I first saw in the early submissions that we received, themes of hopelessness; illustrated by analogies of drowning, being held down and hiding away. These themes very much echoed my own feelings, although hidden even from myself, and perhaps this is why I saw them. The theme of hopelessness is replaced by that of hope; demonstrated by Kulchuma Begum, "*my diagnosis was my lifejacket that helped keep me afloat even in the stormiest of seas*", a diagnosis led to support that she needed and deserved. We are different, not less, and as Diana Katoto tells us, "*...difference doesn't equal failure*".

I now believe, as Deb Solomon explains, "*...despite the challenges, I also am the social worker I am today BECAUSE of my neurotype.*"

I belong here.

REFLECTIONS

Yes, I do want to meet your gecko!

- Vicky Butterfield

Hello, my name is Vicky and I am a social worker who has recently been diagnosed with ADHD. I appreciate you taking the time to read a little of my story. It nearly didn't make it onto this page and it was that struggle that helped me decide to write my experience.

When I was asked to write this piece, I was really excited at the prospect of a new project, a new challenge, something different. I wanted this to be brilliant, informative, witty and well researched. I wanted it to be perfect. I explored what I could write and thought about it for a week straight but it didn't make it to paper. I planned to do it before I went on annual leave. That didn't happen. I planned to do it on the long plane ride to/from Brazil. That didn't happen (shocker!) I got back and planned to do it before the end of the month. That didn't happen. I got Covid and gave up on the idea altogether. I sent the dreaded text of failure: I can't make the deadline, I am sorry but I can't do what I said I would. Adding this text to the lifetime of evidence that I always over commit and underperform I spiralled into familiar negative self-talk; *who did I think I was to believe I could do this? It is my own fault I didn't make the time when I should have, it would be a waste of effort as it would be rubbish even if I did it and I don't have anything valuable to say anyway.* It is only recent, but having a diagnosis has given me the power to begin to reframe these thoughts when they happen and I have a growing crew of neurodiverse folks who 'get it', believe in me and know how to utilise an impending deadline to generate me enough dopamine to get stuff done (thank you Kelly). So here we are.

I was diagnosed with ADHD six months ago. When I received my diagnosis, I was incredibly and deeply sad. I had expected relief, validation, possibly even happiness. Instead, I was full of sorrow for the younger version of me who was taught to think that she was too disorganised, too distractable, not working hard enough, not applying herself, failing to meet her potential, being too bossy, too loud, too chatty, too opinionated. That she was too much. I felt sad for the current version of me that finds it hard to take up space in the world and has never understood why when it seems so easy for others.

Looking back, I feel my diagnosis was missed. My difficulties were not attributed to signs of a physiological difference but simply seen as behaviour. It is hard to express the hurt which occurs when you are measured by the wrong stick. People are harmed when their terrible struggle is perceived as wilful disobedience. When distress is determined to be bad behaviour. When impulsivity is punished as if it is a matter of considered but poor decisions. Mainstream thinking uses rewards and punishment to change behaviour, placing shame at the heart of interactions with undiagnosed neurodiverse people. If you sit quietly, you get a sticker, if you shout out you get detention. If 'you' cannot sit still, then 'you' are the problem and you will be punished repeatedly as if repetition of the same consequence will improve the ability to comply. The result of this constant shaming is that those negative messages are internalised and form the core of self-understanding. My identity formed around the idea that I wasn't good enough because every person I respected had eventually made me feel ashamed of doing things which felt natural and I could not help.

I am lucky to have a wonderful supportive family, and a mum who was a foster carer which exposed me to social work as a profession. Social work has given me an outlet for all the things I was told were 'too much.' Need someone who will amplify the voice of others, lead and be prepared to give a different opinion to others regardless of rank and status? That's me. Need someone who loves to learn, is strong in their conviction, focussed on justice, and will analyse every detail of a situation from every angle to understand what is going on? Here I am. Need someone who overthinks why they are thinking what they are thinking and worries that they might be unintentionally discriminating against others? I am the one for the job. Need someone who has an insatiable thirst for knowledge and is genuinely interested in having conversations about anything no matter how random? Yes, I do want to meet your gecko!

That is not to say that social work is an easy job, and having untreated ADHD has certainly made this a more difficult experience than it needed to be, but I am proud to be a social worker. I love my work which has brought me through child protection, into fostering and adoption and currently in CAMHS. I have worked with the most wonderful people who are doing their best in difficult circumstances – both families and professionals. I have always felt privileged to be invited into peoples lives and walk a part of their journey with them, particularly when working in statutory services when my initial involvement was anything but invited. I now wonder how much of my experiences of feeling different, misunderstood and unfairly judged contributed to my draw to social work as a profession. At the time I did not have a diagnosis to frame my understanding and I feel there is much reflecting for me to do to make sense of these experiences with the knowledge I have now.

What I know for sure is that if I hadn't come into social work, I wouldn't have a diagnosis. I joined CAMHS understanding myself as a useless person who always comes up short and often self-sabotages so my goal is either harder to accomplish or completely impossible. I didn't know that my brain was self-protecting from the pain of a lifetime of harmful messages which blamed me for the impact of neurodiversity. It was meeting my wonderful colleagues in CAMHS who were at times gentle, supportive, *very* honest and always kind hearted which brought me to see myself through a lens of neurodiversity. And once I saw it, it was so obvious. I read somewhere that getting a late diagnosis was like having spent a lifetime trying to do a huge jigsaw puzzle and then finally being handed the lid with the completed picture on the front. This struck me hard, I 'got my lid' aged 37.

Thirty seven years is a very long time to spend not understanding how your brain works. I used to think that feeling relief on the completion of something huge (a degree for example) was typical until I learned that other people feel elated and accomplished. I now know that I have a dopamine deficiency which makes it hard for my executive function to actually *function* so the dopamine reward system doesn't exist for me. Achieving a task gives me the feeling of having held off a disaster for another hour rather than providing evidence to support a sense of worthiness and accomplishment. For me, having untreated ADHD has meant living on the brink of failure. Waiting for 'them' to 'find me out': to see that I am a chaotic disaster zone who has refined the art of deception and created a pretence of capability and knowledge. Prior to diagnosis I started to question this notion when I read the brilliant article 'Stop Telling Women They Have Imposter Sydrome' by Ruchika Tulshyan and Jodi-Ann Burey. Tulshyan and Burey highlight how systems give constant messages which make individuals feel out of place whilst attributing this to individual crises of confidence. The systemic nature of these messages makes it hard to take up space, and even harder to create a space for your neurodiverse self in a neurotypical landscape.

The more the wonderful, well meaning colleagues and managers gave me praise, showed me they appreciated me and held me in good esteem, the more fragile I felt. I was always sure that I had convinced them that I was something I was not, it has only since diagnosis that I have begun to consider that perhaps they were able to see my qualities better than I was. That my view of me was tarnished by years of negative comments, whilst their view was of who I am now, with my knowledge and skills hard earnt from years of practice, education and just showing up to the task every day and doing my best. Most importantly, that showing up and trying my best is *enough*. No one is asking for 'perfection' because perfection is an impossibly high standard I set because of the messages I have internalised about not trying hard enough. I am deconstructing this belief system, but it has been a lifetime in the making and taking it down is going to take time.

Working in social work has taught me much about who I am and my diagnosis been a very significant piece of this puzzle. Being a Social Worker is very much part of my identity and being neurodiverse is becoming embedded too. The two are intrinsically linked and I hope that with my developing understanding I will be a better advocate and more skilled practitioner with the advantage of being positive about neurodiversity both as an ally and as an expert by experience. The opportunities for diversifying into different areas and specialities was a huge draw for me when considering social work and I am grateful for all those I have had and excited for what will come next. I could not have envisaged as a struggling NQSW that ten years later I would be training as a family therapist in CAMHS with a specialist interest in neurodiversity and traumatised children in substitute care. Yet here I am. Imperfect as I am, still showing up and doing my best.

References

Ruchika Tulshyan and Jodi-Ann Burey, https://hbr.org/2021/02/stop-telling-women-they-have-imposter-syndrome]. Accessed February 11, 2021

You Belong Here

- Jenni Guthrie

This article was originally published as a blog on Autistic Social Worker website (www.autisticsocialworker.co.uk) by the author on 6th March 2022

I'm writing this after a difficult but interesting couple of weeks. I'm reflecting on the messages I have tried to share and the messages that keep on coming back to me and my neurokin within a social work context. Although I am referring to Autistic students this message really is a shout out to all neurodivergent students; I guess I don't want to assume I speak for us all.

Because of course I don't.

But this is important to say. And to say it loudly for you to hear. Because it isn't obvious sometimes and everyone needs to hear it.

You belong here. You are valuable. Social Work needs you.

Why am I saying it?

You are a neurotype that oozes that social justice vibe. Whilst no-one has thought about us neurodivergent social workers in terms of research, there is plenty of sources that show we as Autistic people align with a lot of social work values just by being us (Cope and Remington, 2021). Fairness, equity, openness, and rights are high on our agenda for others and often what we strive to seek for ourselves.

And that's another great thing about you. You know. You know what it's like to be different. You may know what it's like to be misunderstood, to stand out, to know hurt. But what's better is that you can use that knowledge to connect. You see it in others, and you understand the need to be understood, heard, and safe. You connect with the trauma experience. You speak the language of surviving.

But there's more

You may see the connections to the connection. What I mean is, you see the detail within the whole picture overview. And that's important. The detail counts. Linking the detail to understand what's going on is an integral strength of the social work role. Analysing, problem solving and really getting deep down into the information is what makes you great. No surface level, skim-reading a person's lived reality here.

And then there's questions. The curiosity. The need to know 'why' as much as the 'what'. To make sure what you are doing is the 'right' thing to do in that context. Its person-centred rather than resource led. Its advocating, challenging with purpose, and not letting that person who you are working to affect change with, fall out of view.

Then there's your commitment. To get things done. To that person who depends on you turning up. To doing a good job. That's a precious ethic to hold. Its builds trust, it enables success (whatever that may look like).

But..........

We have the barriers that prevail and challenge us in holding onto our strengths-based view of ourselves. Imposter syndrome is vicious. It creeps up even when we have succeeded. It makes us question ourselves, our skills, our value. It mocks us when we think we are as good as everyone else in the room. It shuts us down and holds us back.

It holds a lot of power, internalised ableism, fuelled by systemic ableism – those myths and untruths about Autism that are perpetuated between people, teams, organisations, and wider systems.

The sensory overload in a context not designed for us.

This power is hard to challenge, and it can have a massive and harmful impact on our self-esteem, our sense of self our self-worth and even more our self-efficacy i.e., what we believe we can achieve ourselves.

But.........

You deserve those "reasonable adjustments"; you are worthy of those changes you need from others to feel, to respond, to do. To breathe.

You aren't creating a problem; you are illuminating the inequity that surrounds you. In other words, you are highlighting where the problem sits, and accountability towards duty of care. That is where the 'uncomfortable' for others, the ambivalence to see harm resides, not with you.

You are the agent of change in the workplace that can actually make it better for everyone including families) if everyone would just see that. Beyond the normal. Beyond the "it's what we have always done."

So.........

To the Practice Educator who "doesn't have time" to think about what could enable you to thrive in your placement, to the academic assessor who is worried of the "unfair advantage" some extra time may offer in assessment, I challenge you.

To the team manager, the ASYE coordinator, the service manager who questions the need for familiar space; a sense of ownership in the shape of a corner that you can identify when overwhelm is real; or the opportunity to just slow the pace down a smidgen, I challenge you.

Why are you so afraid of change? What is it about "professionalism" you can't see in this social work student who is fighting the onslaught of the day before they even walk into your office. Every single day. Who, despite their trauma, show up. Waiting for you to see the difference their difference is making. And how much yours is restraining them.

And...........

The colleagues who notice, who support, who speak up, we need you. We value you. We thrive and survive with you. You are our secure base.

To our Neurodivergent colleagues and friends, help us create a safe haven where boats rock a little less and the storms are sheltered from. Even just for a little while.

It takes one person to reach out to start building these connections.

And guess what, we are there, in those offices those lecture rooms.

If your organisation doesn't acknowledge and offer space, ask why. Collectively.

And why?

Because you belong here.

You are valuable.

And Social Work absolutely needs you

References

Cope, R. and Remington, A. (2021) The Strengths and Abilities of Autistic People in the Workplace. *Autism in Adulthood*.0(0) DOI: 10.1089/aut.2021.00371

You Belong Here - A message to Student Social Workers, https://www.autisticsocialworker.co.uk/post/you-belong-here-a-message-to-student-social-workers.

What's the point in you if you can't think or do? Reflecting on my Bumpy Journey into Social Work in a Neurotypical World

- Florence Smith

When I sat down to plan my contribution to this book, my mind was bursting with different ideas. My thoughts were moving so fast I couldn't focus on one long enough to hold it. My neurosparkly brain was working its messy magic.

Failing to anchor down one idea, I asked my Dyslexia tutor from my university days for advice. She was excited that neurodivergent social workers were finally being seen.

She asked "what do you wish you saw whilst you were at each step of your journey Florence? Find out and focus on that."

For the next week, my brain whirled as I asked myself that question. I couldn't narrow down what I wish I had when there was nothing to begin with. So, I decided to start with what I thought was the first step, representation.

I wish I had explicitly seen another neurodivergent social worker and had the opportunity to listen to their journey. I wish I had the opportunity to see how they were supported and navigated/challenged the systems around them. I wish I could have absorbed advice and tips from them when I felt out of my depth and felt like quitting. I wish I hadn't felt so alone.

So that is what I hope I can offer to you, a reflective account of my journey to being diagnosed as Dyslexic and Dyspraxic and my journey into social work. A journey which starts in primary school.

I have always 'struggled' academically and never really understood what the aim of school was. This is what I believe prevented my brain from being interested or hooked on learning. Nevertheless, primary school was one of the most positive experiences of my educational life, despite not having a formal diagnosis. At the time this wasn't a problem, I was receiving a lot of help from peers and teachers. The environment they created has been something I have tried to find in different social workspaces.

Although I cannot remember any grammar or spelling rules from primary school, I did learn about the immeasurably positive impact of peer support and belonging. I learnt about support, belonging and acceptance from support groups.

The students who were struggling to grasp the rules of spoken and written English in primary school were invited to a VIP Club... later named the Penguin club where we ate penguin biscuits as rewards! And, of course, we completed extra spelling sheets to help us catch up with the rest of the class. Most of us – although not explicitly stated - were neurodivergent and I began to feel represented and as though I belonged.

The belonging came from creating community, connection and authenticity within the clubs. We celebrated birthdays, we would be excited to learn or get things wrong, we would pair up on work, we could ask for help and we were friends. Importantly we never felt left out or different in this space. I still hold the feelings of belonging and connection close to me.

Looking back, the ease I felt in the groups was because I felt psychologically safe, represented, and included. In trying to take this lesson forward to my present day, these are all factors I look for in workspaces. But I am still learning what this looks like at work and especially in social work.

Unfortunately, a lot of workplaces have felt psychologically unsafe.

However, where I have struggled to find the same sense of community and psychological safety in a workplace, I have found it in the British Association of Social Workers Special Interest Group (SIG). The group gives me that revitalising sense of connection I found in the VIP clubs in primary school. And I often find myself coming out of the meeting and saying to my partner how happy I am that I have "found my people" in social work – just as I had found them in primary school. So my advice to any neurodivergent social worker is to try to find a support group who will help share the load through providing a familiar space, psychological safety, compassion, understanding and being their own neurosparkly selves. And to any managers or senior leaders, please protect these vital spaces for minoritised groups like neurodivergent social workers.

But we better get back to the journey. Although my primary school had a good understanding of my support needs, it was never formalised. Therefore, the support and understanding did not translate into secondary school. After a wealth of support in primary school, moving into secondary school was like jumping in icy cold water after being in a lovely hot sauna. A shock to the system.

Because I had no formal diagnosis, the support I received dropped off a cliff edge. No teachers knew I needed support, or why, and I was not taught what my needs were. Subsequently, I would try to mask my difficulties: I worked harder to try and keep up with my peers, yet found it difficult to stay on task, organise homework, 'apply myself', concentrate or just generally be engaged in what they were teaching me. Socially, I struggled to maintain friendships,

I would hide in the bathroom on lunch so I didn't have to socialise, I would always say "yes" to almost anything, and I struggled to emotionally regulate. But most importantly, I felt alone and as though I was the only struggling student.

This experience - which has been similar to some workplaces – has taught me why I find neurodivergent labels important to gaining formal support and an understanding of yourself.

If I had the formal diagnosis of Dyslexic and Dyspraxic, my secondary school experience might have looked a little bit different. Had I received a diagnosis, I might have known I was neurologically different to my peers which could have stopped me comparing myself to them. I might not have masked, and my self-worth/esteem may have been better. But these are big mights. Maybe wishes for an alternative and inclusive experience.

So my advice from reflecting on this experience is to please try not to see a diagnosis as 'just a label'. Because for some of us, it's a label that could change our support and life. It can validate our experiences and give explanation to why we may do things differently. It could help explain the years of uncertainty, low self-worth, and pain we experience in settings designed for neurotypical brains. A diagnosis or label does not take any of that away. It can, however, bring understanding and give rise to our neurological strengths.

I received a diagnosis of Dyslexia at the beginning of my GCSEs and moved on to study A-Levels. I was proud to have my formal diagnosis and intrigued that they noted 'indications of Dyspraxia'. Equipped with this knowledge, I told my sports teacher I was Dyslexic and possibly Dyspraxic.

"What's the point in you if you can't think or do?" he responded in front of the whole class.

I didn't really understand Dyslexia or Dyspraxia. But the shame and stigma I felt from his stereotype made me want to shed my labels and vanish there and then. He validated internal narratives I developed over secondary school which negatively impacted my self-worth and self-esteem. Worse of all he exposed and shamed me in front of my peers.

Upon reflection, common stereotypes, myths and misconceptions about Dyslexia and Dyspraxia informed his understanding. Which in turn created his opinions which were oppressive, discriminatory, and deficit based. Unfortunately, I didn't learn anything positive from this experience and have no profound learning to share.

The experience is the monster under my bed. When I have wobbles in confidence and am feeling anxious or I am experiencing imposter syndrome, my mind comes straight back to his words.

On the other side of that con, it did/does, however, act as the catalyst to my activism and grit. When I don't feel 'good enough', I remember his words and remind myself he cannot be right. This experience also contributed to my decision to study social work at university. I met social workers who challenged harmful ideas and behaviours - I wanted to do the same.

Whilst applying to university as a first-generation student from a farming family, I felt like my learning needs were a burden. Applying to UCAS, trying to finesse my executive function skills (planning, time management, focus and starting a task etc) and attempting to produce well written personal statements burnt me out. Additionally highlighting the class/economic gap in higher education and access to additional support.

As a first-generation, neurodivergent student attending a financially challenged sixth form, there was:

1. No explicit support I could use to help me with my application, and I didn't have the resources to explore charities online,
2. No signposting from the sixth form as they focused on students with better academic prospects,
3. *No financial support* for the higher education diagnostic assessment,

and as a first-generation student, I could not draw academic support from my family.

My family saved for a diagnostic assessment for higher education. When I received the assessment, the deficit-based language used within the report reflected my inner voice and served as a self-fulfilling prophesy. I was described as; cognitively weak, being cognitively slow, achieving GCSEs *despite* my Dyslexia, being below average and lacking automaticity. I only read one positive comment: I showed determination.

I managed to get the UCAS points to study social work - thank goodness for BTECs with my new formal diagnosis for higher education, I applied for the DSA (Disabled Student Allowance) which enabled me access to assistive computer software, allowance for coloured paper and 36 hours of 1:1 specialist Dyslexia support.

However, whilst I was establishing what support worked for me, I still felt like I was navigating studies in the dark. Not quite grasping academic writing or social rules at university. This was evident in my grades.

I failed my first assignment, and it validated the deficit-based assessment, the comments from my sports teacher and my own negative internal narratives.

However, university wasn't all doom and struggle. Part way through my first year I met a Dyslexia tutor who changed everything. They were the first person to identify positives about Dyslexic thinking which then triggered me to reflect on what I can do. She disrupted and changed the narrative of my story to one of determination, adaptability, and strength.

She helped me realise through her use of language that I had achieved so much despite *standardised systems* working against neurodivergent brains and I had achieved because of the strengths associated with Dyslexia and Dyspraxia.

My Dyslexia tutor showed me new ways of working academically, which drew on what I could do to support my learning instead of dwelling on what was difficult. Upon reflection, she provided a space where I began to really understand that my learning needs do not fit a standardised model. She used images and gave me tips for executive function. She told me to do it my way. She enabled me to stop using term such as 'coping strategies' and instead see it as different ways of working.

Because of her support, the feelings of belonging and safety began coursing through my veins again. I felt seen and accepted for the first time since primary school. I passed my first year of assignments and made it to my first placement.

My first placement was at an adult disability charity – it was an amazing experience. They were curious about and genuinely interested in Dyslexia. They encouraged me to celebrate my neurological difference by writing a piece for their newsletter about being a Dyslexic social worker. They showed me how to break standardised ways of working by supporting me to produce central evidence documents through recorded conversations.

I felt psychologically safe: I could talk to my Practice Educator about my neurosparkly profile, I felt represented as he connected me with other neurodivergent staff and I could say I didn't know how to do something, and they would support me.

My advice to any practice educator out there, please be more like him. Help us thrive and not just survive. Help us change the way systems work so we can work better in them. Help us feel safe being different – being us. And to any student or practicing social workers, find active allies and build relationships with them. Surround yourself with people who empower you and celebrate your difference. These people and these relationships will help you thrive.

My first placement came to an end, I had made leaps and bounds in my professional and personal development. However, after taking one stride forward, I took three strides back on my second placement within a statutory local authority.

I moved from feeling safe and seen to feeling unsafe and unwanted. My practice educator wasn't interested in my neurological needs, they knew I had a diagnosis but did not entertain my discussion about Dyslexia/Dyspraxia and they didn't exercise any curiosity about what this might mean for my practice or learning.

In this environment, I stopped thriving. I struggled with my central evidence documents, to keep up with reading and with executive function skills. My struggles were triggered by the context. I would only be provided with reports minutes before a meeting, instructions were not followed up in writing and protected study time was not honoured (to name only a few).

This was the most difficult time during my studies, and I developed a negative internal narrative. I compared myself to neurotypical students and completely negated my neurological needs. I would have panic/anxiety attacks and I was reluctant to stay on the course.

When I asked for support, they organised an emergency placement meeting with the university and my Dyslexia tutor – not including me. My Dyslexia tutor informed me of the meeting and advocated on my behalf. She was my strength and light.

It was clear from the meeting minutes that my practice educator saw my needs as the problem and making reasonable adjustments difficult within a statutory setting – this validated the comments from my sports teacher and made me feel vulnerable.

If I could have my time again, I would approach the start of my placement very differently. I would have taken more time to reflect on why the first placement worked so well and communicated this with the second placement. I wish I had asserted the need for my practice educator to view my neurological needs and support planning through a social model lens – where we view social constructs as disabling and not the person.

I wish my practice educator took the time to learn about Dyslexia and Dyspraxia, to reflect on the ways our brains might differ and how differences impact the way we think/do. Most of all, I wish she and I were kinder to myself.

I passed the placement with the support of my practice supervisor and Dyslexia tutor. However, I left holding negative experiences of practice and views of my neurodivergence. I was unsure what being newly qualified would look like.

In my first role as a statutory social worker in a children and families assessment team, I met another newly qualified social worker who openly and enthusiastically told me they were Dyslexic. We shared stories of our experiences, good and bad, and really connected. They welcomed me to the team off their own initiative, talking me through the induction period, the assessed portfolio and how to request reasonable adjustments. We supported each other through the year in day-to-day activities too, such as understanding how to write analytical assessments, time keeping, prioritisation and managing our executive function.

This was when I realised, I was not on my own. Despite not knowing other Dyslexic students on my course, not meeting openly Dyslexic social workers on placement and not knowing any academic social workers who are neurodivergent, I was beginning to feel represented. This was when I decided to create the neurodivergent social worker blog.

I wanted to share and extend the positive feeling of representation, belonging and visibility I had in that one workplace and placement. I felt we needed to make space for ourselves as nobody was making that space for us. It is not easy working in a system that is not designed for our way of thinking or being. I wanted social work to start discussing the neurological needs of their social workers. Because of this, I created The Neurodivergent Social Worker website.

Being neurodivergent in social work has been challenging and rewarding. There are times I feel my neurodivergence is a gift and other times it's not. I have left roles I loved because their system did not allow my neurodivergent brain to sparkle, instead it wanted me to fit a mould I couldn't bend to.

I also still make mistakes. I have accepted a job where there were obvious red flags - because it was my passion - only to feel unsupported and unseen. I have grinned and bared sensory overwhelm in the office due to fear of disrupting the status quo, only to burn out at the end of each day. But I now try and be compassionate to myself, I am at the start of my journey and always striving to know better.

So, my final bit of advice is to be kind to yourself. We are trail blazers for the next generation of neurodivergent social workers. We don't have to get everything right first time, it takes time to understand ourselves and what works for us. What is right for one person might not be right for you. Try not to beat yourself up, but make sure that when you know better you can do better and share your learning (if you feel safe).

I like my "strangeness" I think I'll keep it

- Nicola Jordan

My name is Nicola Jordan, I'm a MA social work practice student with the Think Ahead scheme, and I have ADHD.

Being neurodivergent in this area of work I find to be both a challenge and a gift.

It is challenging in the sense that I feel neurodivergence is not understood by many people.

Its presentations, its quirks, its benefits, and the struggles that come with it. The fact that neurodivergent conditions are not homogenous also proves to be a sticking point – due to societal notions of ADHD presenting in a certain way, people may jump to conclusions of who you are as a person, and as a practitioner, based upon assumptions and stereotypes which are often perpetuated in media. At times, I feel a personal urge to overcome these stereotypes and to "prove myself" which is neither useful nor required. I am a whole, interesting, hardworking, and capable practitioner, AND I have ADHD.

I often have a huge sense of imposter syndrome because of my ADHD, feeling that I may lack things my neurotypical colleagues have, or may have, picked up on easier than myself. This can often prompt me to mask my presentation of ADHD. I may appear to understand verbal instruction that I would actually benefit from having written down – yet wanting to appear "normal" and "professional" can imbue a sense of embarrassment when asking for an adjustment such as written instruction.

This sense of embarrassment is not bestowed upon me by my place of work, nor by my university, colleagues, or the people that I work with, rather it comes from implicit bias. I hold myself to such a high standard based on the bias that I hold from a lifetime of both subliminal, and very overt messages about people with ADHD and other neurodiversity. ADHD is more often that not portrayed as a disorder of "mischief" and only within people that have low intelligence. I'm sure we have all seen or heard stories of the "naughty boys" at school with ADHD who disrupt the class and have poor educational attainment. These messages permeate society and are difficult to alter or erase, especially when the condition is a part of you.

There is also the other side of the coin; the perception that to have a neurodivergence means you must also be exceptional in some way. This ideal is also perpetuated by the media – movies such as 'Rain Man' and lists in magazines of "top 10 successful people with ADHD" portraying the disorder as a superpower. This can contribute to a feeling of inadequacy or failure, as though you are not using your "superpower" correctly if you have yet to gain billions in the bank as Richard Branson has. People with ADHD often have a sensitivity to rejection, and this hyperbole may contribute to those feelings. I resent the term superpower, it is not a superpower, nor is it a hindrance. ADHD is just me. I'm just a person who thinks in different ways to you.

I want to be part of the change in the perception of ADHD. I want to encourage colleagues to learn about neurodivergence, to embrace it, to champion the different ways of thinking and working creatively that being neurodivergent can gift you with.

A great benefit I have found, being a neurodiverse social worker, is the ability to pick up on possible neurodiversity in others. Not in such a way as to diagnose them but in being able to relate to people, and to work with them in neurodiverse positive ways. I can provide suggestions to colleagues in formulations on possible ways of working with people which considers their neurodivergence. This can ensure that people receive the support they need and are not so hastily (and problematically) accused of "disengaging" with services.

I also feel a great sense of justice - I have an innate need to attend to the rights of others, to seek justice and fairness for everybody. This is a quirk of being neurodivergent which is very positive when working in social work. This trait strongly supports me in advocating for the people that I work with. I have a passion for human rights and for supporting everybody to live a life they are happy with.

My ADHD supports me to think creatively and to truly consider a holistic approach when working with people. This has enabled me to build effective relationships with the people I work with, colleagues, and other professionals. This helps me to work towards outcomes for people that they are happy with. Masking also plays a part in this. Due to a lifetime of masking to fit in social environments, I can quickly adapt to the situation I am placed in – I can remain calm when in a tense situation, I can use humour effectively to break the ice, and I can build rapport quickly.

In order to succinctly represent my personal experiences with ADHD, I turn to another love - art.

As Francis Bacon said:
"There is no excellent beauty that hath not some strangeness in the proportion"

To be an excellent social worker, I will continue to embrace my neurodiverse "strangeness" and use it to be sensitive to others and the injustices they may experience.

I like my "strangeness." I think I'll keep it.

What If...

- Maximillian Hawker

I was diagnosed with Obsessive Compulsive Disorder (OCD) when I was a child; I'm far from being alone in this respect. The charity OCD-UK estimates that 12 in every 1,000 people in the UK have the condition. That's more than 1 in 100 and represents 1.2% of the population. Just to put that into a bit of context, the National Autistic Society suggests that 1 in 100 people are on the Autism spectrum – so we're talking about comparable numbers here.

OCD is a very misunderstood condition and I may surprise you when I say that, as a *direct* result of OCD, I experience incredibly upsetting and highly intrusive thoughts around violence and sexual violence. 'Oh my God! I thought OCD was about keeping your house tidy. Being a bit of a perfectionist. Hell, it sounds really useful to have it!' I hear some of you say. Where do I even begin with this all-too-common-misnomer? OCD is not a condition simply characterised by perfection, tidying, cleaning, straightening, rearranging, polishing, scrubbing, bathing, vacuuming, dusting, or avoiding cracks on the pavement.

So, what is it then? Let's break down the term itself.

- **The O stands for obsessive.** That means you can't stop thinking about something, no matter how hard you try. More than that though, you're thinking about something that's really upsetting you.
- **The C stands for compulsive.** That means you are compelled to do something to alleviate your anxiety

because your obsessions are uncomfortable at best and panic-inducing at worst.

- **The D stands for disorder.** That means that something's wrong. We all get nonsensical, weird little thoughts and most of us can ignore them. With OCD, however, that mechanism of logic is broken and we can't stop dwelling on those thoughts.

How do you know if someone has OCD? How would you know that I have OCD? Well, you can't *see* my OCD because it happens in my brain. Sometimes, some of my compulsions involve a physical action, such as the incessant hand-washing demonstrated by Jack Nicholson's character in *As Good As It Gets*, or the tidying and cleaning by Tony Shalhoub's titular detective *Monk*. But that is not the case most of the time. Most of the time, OCD is the very definition of a hidden illness.

As have other OCD sufferers, I've learned to disguise my compulsions. The go-to compulsion for me is reassurance-seeking, which is a subtle and effective way of trying to relieve the anxiety of an obsession. Typical reassurance-seeking behaviour can typically involve repeatedly checking something (e.g. making sure a gas hob is definitely switched off, or watching the local news for any mention of yourself having committed a crime) or asking a trusted person for some guarantee or assurance that your obsessive thought is not something to worry about. I, for instance, have become adept at subtly dropping things into conversation to try and illicit a desired response from someone that will give me the reassurance I crave.

Please disregard any notion you may have that OCD is in any way helpful or twee. There is nothing cute, quaint or charming about OCD – it is not a soft-haired bunny with an irresistible face and it is in no way something you want to have. It is a serious condition that often requires psychological treatment and can be really damaging to the sufferer if left untreated. Imagine if you had irrational, terrifying thoughts flying around your head all day that made you feel like you were always on the edge of some impending disaster. Sound good? Nope. It is not fun or helpful and it demands understanding as opposed to mockery. It certainly merits far more training for practitioners in the fields of both health and social care.

A lot of research and studies have been conducted to try and work out where OCD comes from. At the moment, it looks like a number of things can lead to a diagnosis, but there is no definitive answer. We do know that OCD runs in families, however, and that points to it possibly being a genetic disorder. Research also suggests that OCD involves a problem with two parts of the brain 'talking' to each other: the front part of the brain and some of the deeper parts of the brain. Further research involving scans of the brains of OCD sufferers has shown interesting structural differences when compared with people who don't have OCD. So, in this respect, we can say that if you have OCD, you are neurodivergent. Whether it is an acquired form of neurodivergence or not – as opposed to something you are born with – is a separate matter that continues to present a rich vein for academic curiosity.

Now, imagine having the anxiety associated with OCD while also practising as a social worker. Yeah, it's not fun, but that's my reality.

Social work is a difficult job as it is without the added pressure of having my brain trying to undermine me at every turn. Intrusive images of harming people are distressing beyond words, but the effects of OCD do not begin and end there.

Here are some of the other ways it impacts me:

- **Mood.** I can be relatively happy one moment and then, the next, I'm incredibly low and struggle to summon the enthusiasm or energy to do anything. I think I'm difficult to be around for colleagues in the workplace as they are always second-guessing how I'm feeling from one day to the next. It therefore impacts my ability to be a team player. My anxiety is elevated at all times, so every day I'm obsessively preoccupied with all manner of things that can go wrong – in social work, that's quite a lot!
- **Scrupulosity.** A real issue I have is the amount of time and effort I give to every task I have to complete. There is a strong element of scrupulosity in OCD – far more perverse than mere perfectionism – and it means that I have to give one-hundred percent to every single thing I do, else I worry about how it reflects on me or whether I've made a mistake that may adversely affect those I support. I then ruminate about it and revisit it until I'm happy with my efforts. As you may imagine, when I have assessments, plans, reports and case notes coming out of my ears, I find time management to be a real problem, as I have to give my all to everything I do. Sure, it means that my standard of work is high, but it comes at a personal cost.
- **Career.** Another problem I have is that, long-term, I struggle to see myself getting very far in social work. Simply being a case-working social worker is demand enough on my mental health, and I really don't know how I would cope in positions of greater responsibility. My career, therefore, is finite and I regularly consider alternatives. I simply won't go far in this line of work and that saddens me deeply.

I look at other neurodivergent people and I see how they find strength in the ways they are different. I'm really happy for them, but I feel sad for myself and others like me who are also different but don't want to be different. Of course, if I didn't have OCD then I would be a different person altogether. I like to think there are good things about me that might be connected to my diagnosis, but I can't help but wonder as to who I could have been without OCD.

At the moment, my OCD is more manageable than it's ever been, as I've persevered with cognitive behavioural therapy (CBT), medication, and have a sort of stubborn resolve to not be beaten by this damn thing. However, I remember all too clearly the times when my OCD was at its most severe and I simply couldn't get out of bed – I was tearful, suffering with panic attacks, exhausted, and struggling to see a reason to continue living. My obsessive theme of violence and sexual violence is ideally suited to cause me maximum distress, as I survived childhood abuse myself and watched my siblings suffer abuse too, so it's something that upsets me on a very instinctive level. OCD has an insidious habit of 'picking' the thing that will upset a sufferer most and trying to convince them that they are something they aren't: a monster capable of terrible things. For me, the thing I find most objectionable is the idea of harming a child, so my OCD tries to convince me that I am someone who could do that. In this respect, OCD is often likened to a malign entity that is almost intelligently focused on the sufferer's destruction. It doesn't *actually* talk to you – you don't hear voices – but you're aware of its presence and its message. It's how I imagine John Hurt might have felt in the movie *Alien*. However, the very fact that you are distressed by the thoughts you have is evidence that you are *not* the monster your OCD wants to make you out to be; a real monster would enjoy such thoughts.

The intrusive thoughts themselves can take different forms. Sometimes, I get very crisp images of me doing something terrible. Sometimes, I get a sense or an intuition of an event occurring without a concrete image. Alternatively, I might simply have an emotive impression in my mind: so, a feeling of self-loathing at the thought of hurting someone. The most spectacular thoughts are 'false memories.' As the term suggests, this is when you are convinced that you can recall a memory of having committed some horrendous act or crime, and all you are left with is disgust and a fear of being 'caught'. Of course, the memory itself is a lie, but it seems bloody real. As a child, I had false memories of throwing rocks off of motorway bridges into oncoming traffic and killing people. I used to check newspapers and websites for details of such events (reassurance-seeking.) Naturally, I never found any records, but I was utterly convinced I'd committed the act. In psychiatry circles, such themes in OCD are called 'repugnant obsessions' – for good reason, I might add! There is an unsettling quality to them that people are afraid to discuss for fear of condemnation. But none of us control our thoughts, and if the circuitry in our brains is misfiring then perhaps we shouldn't be ashamed of that. We need understanding.

In closing, I hope I've given you a taster of what OCD is really like, and I would implore you to bear in mind at least some of what I've said when you encounter colleagues and service users with the condition. After all, social work is challenging enough without the added surrealism of OCD.

At the age of 35, I entered a world that was full of new things

- Deb

I was unable to read and write until I was 35 years old, I was asked to leave school at 14, and I was that child who would be hidden away when school inspectors arrived.

However many years later, after experiencing homelessness and other barriers to moving forward, I finally found the strength to leave Edinburgh, and found myself under the guiding and safe wing of my Dad.

I attended Learn Direct and started to focus on me... I learnt to read and write, and completed level 1 and 2 literacy and numeracy... I had no clue that this was equivalent to GCSE.

I was extremely happy.

Moving forward a few months, I was sat on a seat at Teesside university, studying for a Youth Work and Youth Studies degree. I was failing, but still no clue about Dyslexia.

A lecturer picked up some patterns in my writing and before long I was being assessed for Dyslexia.

The day I was told I had Dyslexia, I was heartbroken, I thought that I would be removed from the programme.

Once support and strategies were put in place, my grades went from 30% to 55 then up to 75%. I passed my 1st degree with a 2.1 I was ecstatic.

I then worked as a youth worker for a while, then wanted to support others who battled with Dyslexia.... I knew that if I done this, others could too.

I then achieved a Merit for PGCE and then in what feels like a blink of an eye, I was on the Step Up to Social Work programme.

Here I sit today, in a role that I feel privileged to be in, and sit here writing with confidence that I have the ideal skills to do the role that I love, but I still have moments of panic, the panic is due to writing complex reports, or doing any written court work. I still struggle but have come so far in a short space of time.

From homelessness till 2008 to sit here as a qualified social worker in my 2nd year of ASYE.

Whilst in the role, I was aware of the numerous NQSW that were starting that also had Dyslexia.

I asked if I could create a role to offer support, a guidance so to speak to guide NQSW through the what can be complex steps to get the right support in place.

I share with parents, tips and tricks to access support, I share details with other professionals and IROs, on how to use free resources and how to work smarter not harder.

However, the barriers are still there, I struggle when asked questions in court, so now I make sure that all advocates are aware that I have Dyslexia. This enables me to have time to think and be asked questions in a different way.

I have struggled, but I have ensure that I am solution focused.

I find ways to think outside the box, I am told that I am creative in the direct work I do and I feel that I am proud to be where I am, despite the Dyslexia.

Being neurodiverse in social work is not easy, colleagues may need 1 run around the block to do the same tasks that take me 6 runs around the block (hope that makes sense)

Dyslexia is not who I am, but I am proud to be Dyslexic as it has made me the creative person I am. Yes I struggle, but getting the right tools in place will help.

To focus on my ASYE year and the challenges faced with having Dyslexia.

Starting out as NQSW was scary, imposter syndrome was intense, so much so I'd allocated it a name... SWAT... SWAT was with me daily, it was becoming a constant in my life. I'd find myself focusing on SWAT, and forgetting about the stuff I do well. SWAT stands for Scared & Worried About This... Not very creative I know but hey... SWAT was also hard work.

No puns intended here, but I'd find my self trying to swish away SWAT, or swat the SWAT and trying again... But each day SWAT returned.

Being terrified I'd get it wrong, feeling nervous about sharing my opinion or views... Swatting daily.

As an NQSW who is neurodiverse (Dyslexia) I found myself very much like rabbit in headlights.

However, I'd keep sharing my love for the role, I'd hear myself encouraging others to apply for social work and I'd often share how much I **REALLY** do love the role, feeling privileged to do the role and having mini successes with families, all of these things helped with SWAT.

But then it would ALWAYS return, with an annoying buzz in my working day... And sometimes it would appear on weekends, you know those **rare days** that we get to switch off and recharge... Yes? Those days would have a hefty dollop of SWAT.

The support from the social work academy overall was fantastic. It helped me refocus and turn down the annoying buzz from SWAT.

I STILL have struggles, but I have strengths too.

I have areas to develop but I've got areas where I'm doing well.

Ofsted came earlier in the year, and I was feeling very emotional when a young boy who I'm working with wrote a letter to Ofsted... He'd added *"life is better now than it was before... & Debbie is annoying at times when she asks lots of questions ☺"* he wrote that he felt listened to and other nice bits too... and a 10 year old who tells me she's the safest she's felt in a long time, and says thank you for helping her mummy get help... When a mum of 3 calls me to say *"Hi, I just wanted to say thank you for your help, I feel like I have been able to get stuff out, get help and my kids are doing better now, thank you"*... Don't get me wrong, there's still a lot of people who do not feel like the role I do, or steps they are asked to take.. Sometimes I get called names but I've learnt that it's not personal...

I remind myself **WHY** I do this role. I do not just want to make a difference; I want to be the difference.

There were times where I was worried about the ASYE portfolio, worried it would not pass, but this was partly due to my old friend SWAT, which coupled with my Dyslexia bopping me about a bit, things were rough at times.

I'm not saying SWAT has left the building (yet) but it knows where the door is.

I'm sat here today aware of my strengths and aware of areas to improve on. I'm confident in my role, I finally believe that I am in the right role, **for the right reasons**. Not every day is easy, but learning to slow down, and do one task at a time... All helps.

If I could give any social work student any advice, it would be...

Self doubt is going to happen, but try not to let it cloud the skills you have.

Self doubt is greedy, the more you feed it, the bigger it grows... Learn to starve it and get ready to flourish. ☺

ND Me

- Sam Keeton

I currently work with some of the best social workers you can find. They are not only kind and understanding towards those we serve, but also towards each other. I'm not just talking those of us at the bottom (though I often get confused if as a Team Manager I am still "at the bottom") but all the way up to the guy at the top.

This kindness and understanding has been vital to my progression as a social worker.

The understanding shown to me by my manager when I ask for clarity, or less vagueness, or to explain something again in a different way, or to put up with my constant, hard to follow talking whilst I reflect over a situation. It's vital, I cannot manage without it. My anxiety can make life crippling at times, I need this space and understanding.

It's not always been this way though. I recall times where I have been "told off" by a former manager for not giving her what she is demanding of me, even though I have explained I don't understand or have what she is demanding and have asked for a different explanation. Or times I have been given vague instructions and have therefore not done "what was asked", leading to more telling offs. This lack of understanding led me to feel like I was worthless, stupid and led me to seek professional support. I had workplace counselling, it was vital to getting me through that period of my career, a period which could had seen the end of my career, and I can't thank her enough for helping me see my ND brain was not the problem.

My ND brain is treated as an asset where I am now. The way I collect, organise and store useful information. The way I have devised easier ways for others to collect and store their information and the way I have created detailed yet simplistic guides to help others with their learning or using new systems.

This is not to say it's all plain sailing. Being Neurodiverse in a largely Neurotypical world is hard. I have had to create complex systems to be able to retain quickly given important information, particularly when given over the phone. It takes me much longer to grasp things around me. I have the most amazing team, who are accepting and understanding of my ND, we joke about our shared struggles, my memory being a key one, as a member of my team also has memory difficulties, and we often joke about how when we both have a "bad day" conversation (or lack thereof) can be brilliant.

"err, no it was last week wasn't it"

"nah I'm sure it was yesterday"

"who was it about again"

"agh I've forgotten"

Then I check my details and comprehensive logs and we're back on track, and we laugh, and we manage to carry on doing our jobs in the best way.

I love social work.

This is vital, as my brain, when I love something, has a drive to just keep learning, and I soak it up like a sponge, dedicating hours to learning more. The passion then spills over into my team and they too carry that passion in everything they do, fighting for the rights of those we serve, striving to make the world a better place, one intervention at a time. I'm sure that the discrimination I have faced in my life has created the drive in me to address that discrimination and inequality head on, and it's what keeps me going, every day. I also feel it makes me more empathetic, I understand the pain of being given bad instruction, or being treated badly because of a perception that I should be or think a certain way. I won't do that to my team.

I've been told time and time again that I have "the best way" of teaching and explaining things. This is because I need to take significant time and effort to learn the details of something, and when I am confident, I am able to convey this to whoever needs it in a really simple way, as this what was needed for my brain to understand it. I think in colour and metaphor and musically; which, at least for the former two, it seems most people love to be taught in, I've learnt most people don't usually like to be sung to.

I put huge pressure on myself (as I know many other ND people do) to not let those around me down, to behave more Neurotypical: to not be bothered by the clashing perfumes, bright buzzing lights or chatter in the office, to rehearse simple conversations so when needed I can respond "normally."

Though, in large part to working somewhere I am more able and free to be me, I have started unmasking a bit. Where I am struggling I have started to say this, when I notice I am having a bad brain day I say this, If I can't join in a conversation I have (in most part) stopped trying, or nodding along, and have started saying "yeah I have no knowledge of this subject so I'm going to step out," often this produces a safe laugh as my team understand me, and that I mean no offence.

I still try to keep up with everyone else in less safe situations. I have been known to ask unusual questions, I don't always understand "the joke," I struggle in conversation I know little about and over talk/share in conversations that I do.

I am very trusting (can be a bit naive) and have been taken advantage of many times in my career, it has often taken deep reflection and taking time to realise this. Then I often feel bad for not seeing it sooner, and it means even more time I need to dedicate to be able to keep up with my peers.

Social Work in this country at the moment is scary. I am finding I am very tired. I feel a deep urge and desire to help fix the problems of the country. In university I recall saying I wanted to change the world, and often being laughed at for it, but the world is different through each set of eyes, and If I can make it better for one person, I have changed the world.

I cannot fix the country, or the world, but my ND brain creates an enormous pressure to try.

My hope from writing this reflection, is to give a slight glimpse into how I feel my ND brain impacts on my practice, and where things are improving, and maybe, someone reading this might feel less alone, or may change their practice to be just a bit more understanding of their ND colleagues.

Autism: Reflecting on Being Diagnosed in Adulthood

- *Amanda P.*

I had two assessments, one in my 20s and one in my 30s. Both were very different experiences and had two different outcomes. The questions of whether it is worth having the assessments at all, and whether a diagnosis would even matter, were ones I struggled with, and sometimes still do.

On some level, it clearly did matter otherwise I wouldn't have asked for the second assessment, even if it was just to quiet that voice in my head that spent the intervening decade asking if they had really got it right the first time.

Going ahead with having an assessment for Autism as an adult is a bit of a lottery, unfortunately. My first one was done privately, arranged by my university. I wasn't stuck on a waiting list for months or years, but I was never totally comfortable with it because it felt like any other assessment I'd had with a psychiatrist. Except for his opening observation that my choice of career made it unlikely I was Autistic, that was.

The first time Autism was mentioned to me, I was surprised, but more than anything, confused. Not necessarily because it was being suggested at all - although I desperately wished it wasn't - but if I did have it, surely it would have been picked up earlier? It's not like I'd never been accused of being a bit weird/strange/not quite right before.

Even I wouldn't have described myself as normal, but by that age I thought I had some sense of myself, of who I was or at least who I wanted to be - in my case, to be honest, I just wanted to be like anyone else. Average. And yes, normal. Whatever that is.

So, being told that people thought I might be Autistic was quite a shock, and at the time felt almost like an accusation, especially the way it was initially delivered, as a passing comment about my personality.

How could I have reached my mid-twenties with nobody picking up on the fact there might actually be a diagnosable condition present, especially taking into account the amount of mental health professionals I'd been in contact with over the years? The thought that those things that I always saw as just a bit strange might actually be signs of neurodiversity was hard to comprehend. On one hand, that would mean it wasn't my fault. But it also meant it wouldn't be going away.

I dismissed any concerns at first, terrified of the potential (or imagined) implications of a diagnosis, so I was relieved by the outcome. But that little voice was there, asking if I was sure. Was I really, completely, honest in response to the questions? Or was I, consciously or not, stopping short of giving answers deep enough to tell the total truth?

At some point I realised the only way to be sure was to ask for another assessment, but it took me several years to bring myself to do it. I knew it would be difficult. The assessment process includes questions about childhood, development, communication and relationships. It's intrusive.

So, after a referral from my GP, there was a year on a waiting list and then two Covid-enforced virtual appointments, with an occupational therapist followed by a speech and language therapist. It proved to be a much more in-depth process than previously, and that time, the computer (a literal computer programme) said yes. Diagnosis.

Getting a diagnosis didn't change who I am, it just put a label on and/or provided an explanation for different aspects of me, depending on which way you look at it.

It did have an impact on how I view myself, and how I see myself within the world around me. However, giving a name to something recognises that there is a something. Something other people share. An explanation for that social awkwardness or why I can cope with something one day and not the next.

I can't help wondering what would have happened if I had been diagnosed in childhood, or when I was first assessed. Maybe everything would have been different. Maybe nothing would have been. Maybe it was better this way, when I was in control of the decision and ready to find out for certain. I'll never know, and thinking that way just gets very confusing, very quickly.

As far as my choice of career goes, well, I'm not the only person in these fields with Autism. Awareness is increasing and stigma decreasing everyday.

These careers are stressful. However, supervision and CPD are standard. Additional support can also be sought. With insight, honest reflection, and being willing to ask for and accept help when required, there is no reason why a successful career in this field should not be possible.

Running on marbles

- Deb Solomon

I have been working for my local authority since I qualified as a Social Worker in 2018 at the age of 41, when I was excited to begin my new career. Working in a busy office, I have always received comments such as "Oh you are so organised". I am the Queen of 'To-Do' lists; everything is written down and planned. And colour coded. I thought that was because I was just that kind of person. At home though, I lost my keys constantly. Forgot PE day for the kids. Had to check 20 times where I was going for a visit because I had forgotten the address. And I was exhausted.

Then Covid and lockdown hit. Working from home, I found myself getting less and less organised, staring into space, desperately trying to get my brain working, but somehow failing. The harder I tried, the worse it became. The 'To-Do' lists were overwhelming, I would 'freeze' for hours, unable to do anything, in tears and feeling totally incompetent. I could see my colleagues struggling with the isolation of lockdown, but they seemed to be getting through work, whereas I felt I was always playing catch up. The way I would describe it was like being in a race where everyone else was running on a track but I was running on marbles – never quite getting to the finish line but always putting in double the effort and feeling exhausted. Worrying that it was the depression I had been previously diagnosed with worsening I booked an appointment and was shocked when I was told I had Attention Deficit Hyperactivity Disorder (ADHD). I am an introvert, the quiet one gazing out the window daydreaming.

This I soon learnt is a classic sign of ADHD in women.

My diagnosis led me to research the condition, especially in adult women as I knew very little about it. As I read, everything fell into place. Struggling to focus, hyperfocus at times, time blindness and disorganisation, forgetfulness, impulsivity, emotional dysregulation. The list goes on. Where I had been the "Queen of To-Do lists" that was actually my way of getting through the day. Without that, I couldn't manage. While I have always been successful, working from home, alone for a long period of time has been a whole new challenge and required me to come up with a new set of coping strategies.

This also led me to think about the people we support with ADHD. I had never considered how I approach my working practice with this kind of neurodivergent condition, but now I felt I needed to really consider the person-centred approach and how successfully I applied it – can that person listen to a whole list of things over the phone, or should I send it in a letter? If they miss an appointment – it could be they really have tried to attend, but that day it just wasn't possible. A person within an abusive relationship may find it more difficult to leave considering the low self-worth and confidence – an unfortunate symptom of ADHD.

Researching ADHD in adults has now become a real interest, both in terms of supporting service users and also our profession. I started a national group for neurodivergent social workers, as although I have spoken to many since my journey began, there was no such support group available in the UK. Adult ADHD especially in women is so under researched and misdiagnosed, it is so important to start shining the light on this neurotype, not only the difficulties but also the skills and strengths that comes with it.

Now it sounds like I now have it all figured out after my diagnosis. However, I absolutely don't. I have gone through the 'Change Curve' as described by Kubler-Ross many times (Kubler-Ross 1969). The curve provides a perspective on what we go through in the process of any change and includes the phases of shock, denial, frustration, depression, acceptance and integration. Feeling the loss and anger at what could have been different had I known, to feeling inspired and energised after being amongst other neurodivergent social workers in our meetings can make it an emotional rollercoaster. But it feels very much like a journey, sometimes I feel like I have all my ducks in a row, some days it feels like my ducks have left me completely.

What I have noticed is that I am kinder to myself. For so many years I worked on the hypothesis that everyone else was working harder/better/quicker than me. I can recognise that the impact of going undiagnosed is the unrealistic expectations I place on myself. I recognise that my executive function has good and bad days, but overall it evens out. I also recognise that despite the challenges, I also am the social worker I am today BECAUSE of my neurotype.

As time goes on, I have to re-evaluate my own expectations. I never understood the ebb and flow of need and spent a long time feeling frustrated that I can't always function as I want to. I am continually questioning myself, and the blame I feel is sometimes overwhelming. Are my children really neurodivergent or is it because they have grown up with me as their parent? Do I really have ADHD or am I just no good at my job? What is my personality and what are just traits of my neurotype? But having the diagnosis allows me to rationalise these thoughts before they embed themselves.

Setting up our UK group for neurodivergent social workers has given me purpose and focus and the peer support is invaluable. I still very much have days where I struggle to pull my thoughts together and the meetings can become a little unstructured, however coming together to support each other, have a unified voice and the ability to make real changes to our profession for the next generation of social workers is priceless. Seeing the emotions on a member's face when they realise they are not alone makes all the self-doubt worth it. And so, we will carry on as a collective voice, picking each other up when we need, making noise when it's required and creating that space to be our whole selves, celebrating the wonderful diversity in our profession.

We need to celebrate and embrace our different ways of working and thinking! In the meantime, as social workers it's important that we remember to take care and be kind to ourselves to enable us to do the amazing work we do every day. We encounter problems, but we are NOT the problem!

References

Kubler-Ross, E (1969). On Death and Dying. (New York) Macmillian.

The Neurodivergent SWan

- Katie Küken

When I was 10 years old, my mum – a trainee teacher at the time - marched into my primary school and told my teacher that I would not be completing the additional homework being set to "prepare" me for the year 6 SATs exams. I remember my teacher reassuring my mum "Katie is a high performer; she will be fine" (being a "high performer" will be something I go on to struggle with forever). Sticking to her guns, my mum again made clear there would be no completing extra homework because "I'm not having her in that state again!"

That state was a state I adopted throughout my entire education journey, and into my professional life. It is the feeling that my thinking abilities move from the fluid colours, pictures, shapes and ideas I generally experience, to very suddenly drowning in treacle when faced with tasks I can't picture or predict. The treacle is debilitating. I become messy, emotional, panicked. Hypersensitive to any noise. Hypersensitive to my own mess – the literal mess I'm constantly making. Unable to describe to anyone what I'm going through, I withdraw. To those I cannot withdraw from I am tearful, sometimes angry, and working from the moment I wake up until there is no choice but bedtime. I won an award in year 6 for "a mature approach to SATs exams"... my first reward for pushing myself to the brink to avoid talking about what I found difficult.

It wasn't until I was sixteen that I was formally diagnosed with Dyslexia and Dyspraxia after it was picked up during a compulsory entrance exam I had to sit for college. I was invited back for an assessment with an Educational Psychologist... "what absolute nonsense... I'm high performing!"... I attended nonetheless and began to panic halfway through the assessment. There were exercises I could not comprehend; some I could not complete. I felt panicked. I felt angry. At the end I sat down with the Educational Psychologist who said "I have established you do have Dyslexia and Dyspraxia and have developed very strong coping mechanisms over the years" ... I duly burst into tears and refused all support offered.

I went home, still tearful, and apologetically told my parents – both secondary school teachers by this time. They were supportive, understanding, and encouraged me to accept whatever help I could get. Pride... or misunderstanding?... prevented me from accepting any help until university. I was born and grew up in Tower Hamlets, East London, and had been considered one of the smart kids. A move out of London into a new college introduced me to new challenges – people assuming I was stupid because of my accent, large class sizes, and no friends (turning me in to a prime bullying target.) This on top of my brand-new diagnosis of "not being very good at learning" saw me, for the first time in my academic life, as a *cause for concern* with poor attendance and disengagement in lessons. I never floated in that college and returned to my East London school sixth form for the final year of A Levels. The long-term relationships with the teachers and my peers there, and the smaller classrooms, meant that I was able to revert comfortably back in to my "high achiever" status, though my final A Level results will always be a reminder of the year I couldn't ask for help.

I had an excellent history teacher who convinced me to access all the support offered for Dyslexia and Dyspraxia once I went to university. Whilst not all the support was useful for me and my "very strong coping mechanisms", adjustments such as extra time in exams and sitting in a separate, less stimulating room meant I did not experience the usual debilitating panic of exams. I saw the benefit of reaching out for and accepting help, and continued to do so, until I overheard a peer accusing me of "faking it" and attributing my good marks to "special treatment". Whilst I didn't believe them – I know from open discussion that I experience things differently to many people – that "high achiever" did not want her hard work discredited. So, I returned to the withdrawing, the tears, the panic, the endless hours of work. I thought to myself that I only really needed to get through two more years of a degree, and this would never be an issue again.

Dyslexia and Dyspraxia came with its own set of difficulties as a social work professional. I learned my "strong coping mechanisms" are all based in academia – this is all they had been measured against before. Now there were new challenges; organising a diary for me and my caseload; writing care plans, risk assessments, reports and remembering to include everything; presenting to mental health review tribunals and using the right words; finding my words; being on time; constantly getting lost on the way to new places; having no choice but to learn how to drive and then of course, the constant stress around parking. Key performance indicators became a source of great anxiety. Much about the organisational pressures of this job became a source of great anxiety. The only time I felt at ease, and good at my job, was when I was working directly with people. Dyslexia and Dyspraxia aren't doom and gloom diagnoses, you see, there are strengths. Adults with Dyslexia are said to possess a strong sense of empathy for others and high levels of motivation and determination, especially for problem solving – and these are strong social work skills.

Unlike Educational settings, Health and Social Care Services do not have clear, embedded support options and policies for those with diagnosed learning differences, instead we are asked to single ourselves out as different. I was met with patronising tones, offered 'Dragon Speak' and warned this could take months. Instead of pushing, I started to redesign my "strong coping mechanisms" to fit in with a role as a social worker. This again involved long hours and often spending the evenings on my own in the office, not letting on that I was struggling.

So, I became a high performer as a social worker and viewed as capable of managing a complex caseload. My caseload went from 14 (during my first qualified year) to 20... to 25... to 30... to 38... to 45... to 52. It was at 52 (a number which still haunts me) that things unravelled. I was endlessly making lists and losing them, planning my time out in a diary, and then losing the diary. I had recurring dreams about crashing my car. I withdrew from those I could withdraw from. I was difficult to live with... but no one at work could know – I did not want to look stupid, like I couldn't cope. I daren't ask for support, I daren't ask for *special treatment*. I look back now and wish I could tell myself then that I was not coping because my caseload was far too high – even for a neurotypical social worker – and that my overcompensation was because of a broken system, not because of any shortcomings in me. This went on for months until I lost my purse one morning and it was looking like I'd get into the office on time, rather than an hour early. A small incident in comparison to the emotional labour involved in my caseload at the time, on top of admin work, but this was the *straw that broke the camel's back*. That morning, my mum appeared and told me in no uncertain terms that I was not going to work, because we were going to the doctor. I did not return to work for two months.

I do not think my experience of burning out is solely a result of neurodivergence, but I do believe two months of sickness could have been avoided had there been an environment which better catered for those who are neurodivergent. When I returned to frontline social work - armed with an occupational health assessment that didn't say much and the invaluable support and understanding of social work colleagues - I developed my confidence working in different teams; I became an AMHP (Approved Mental Health Professional), then a Senior Practitioner, then a Consultant Social Worker, and now a Practice Lecturer in a university. During this time, I have discovered that diagnoses of Dyslexia and Dyspraxia do not highlight an inadequacy in me but are a reminder that I think, *and do*, differently – I now mostly see this as a strength. That is not to say that this progress has come easily, I still struggle – there have been tears, mess, anger – but I am now far more skilled in communicating with colleagues about how I feel, and this has made a difference.

Thinking back to the day I received my diagnoses; I never would have thought I would be so accepting as to talk and write openly about this subject. Time, experience, and a great deal of emotional encouragement have taught me that being open and asking for help and support only provides further opportunities to enjoy my work. I hope to one day see public sector workplaces creating safe spaces for their neurodivergent workforce. Spaces where we are firstly *believed*, but more than that, we are offered support in the same way educational settings are expected to provide support for their students. Currently, it seems, we are left to fall from a cliff edge – not all of us with a safety-net-mum.

Circus

- Kelly Bentley-Simon

Sometimes I feel like I'm a one-person circus. I'm walking a tightrope; one wrong step and everything will come tumbling down. Other days, I'm a trapeze artist, gracefully flying through the air. The ground comes rushing towards me, dangerously close, my heart thumping, but it's ok, I know exactly what I'm doing. The crowd ooh and aah, "How do you do it?" they say, "that's amazing!"

I shrug, can't everyone do this? I'm not bothered by the stunts, the lions and the cannons, they don't phase me. It's the other bits, the "easy" things.

I like to project a certain image of myself. In fact, I'm so good at doing it, that at times I don't even realise. Occasionally, this is helpful, but often it's not. I know that I often appear calm and unbothered, and perhaps because of this I don't get the help I might need. This is especially difficult in situations where I'm uncomfortable or where I'm struggling. If I don't realise that I need help, and I don't look like I need help, how likely is it that I will receive help? I'm not great at maths, but I know the odds aren't high.

This is something that I'm still working on, trying to remember that I don't need to struggle, that its ok to be a bit slower with some things and asking for help is definitely ok.

I was diagnosed with Dyscalculia in my late 20's and ADHD in my late 30's. I did relatively well at school, passed all of my

GCSE's without really trying (even Maths), and just about passed my A-Levels, even though I tried really hard.

It took me until I was 40 before I finally finished university and earned a degree. I've previously earned a Certificate of Higher Education (Education Studies), a Diploma of Higher Education (Youth and Community Studies), and a whole degree level module with the Open University, before finally earning a BA in Social Work.

I currently work as a social worker in a multidisciplinary child and adolescent mental health team. I work directly with children and young people carrying out Autism and ADHD assessments, contributing to the diagnostic decision making and feeding back to families, schools and other professions about any decisions made. The work that I'm doing alongside the team is leading me to think I might be more neurodivergent than I first thought. Plus, I'm learning more about how my brain works and I think this can only be a good thing, even though it's a really difficult thing to process.

I often think about the positives that being neurodivergent brings. I've been told many times that I relate well to people who are often seen as "difficult to engage" or "hard to reach." I think maybe it's because neurodivergent people *are* a little different, we see and experience things that others often don't. I regularly find myself stepping back to analyse a situation. What's happening, how has this happened, what might happen next, what might help? When I started studying social work, this approach felt very natural to me, I wondered why it was being taught. Wasn't this something everyone could do? My brain naturally makes links between subjects, not linear connections, but entwined, tangled ones. Connections that only I can understand, a bit like when a parent might suggest a bedroom is messy, except I know exactly where everything is, ordered chaos.

Sometimes, my brain is amazing, I love to learn new things and I pick new skills up easily, I can try my hand at many things and be decent at most of them, but some things I struggle with every time, like I'm learning them for the first time. Anything to do with numbers takes me a long time. Starting any kind of task can be impossible and if I'm interrupted doing something difficult, there's almost zero chance of me being able to pick up where I left off. It's like closing a book without a bookmark, what page was it? Have I read this bit? Wait, this page is too far on, none of this makes sense. How long have I spent looking for my place now? I can't remember what I've read, I'm sure I should be doing something else...but right now, I need to focus.

The lights go down and the show starts, I am the master of ceremonies, the lion tamer, and the clown. I am flying on the trapeze, breathing fire, and watching from the audience.

I am the whole circus, the big top and everyone in it. It's exhausting, but tonight is a sell out and the show must go on!

Corona Diploma

- Kennith Roulston

I am currently a social work student going into my third year of a four-year undergraduate course. I have temporal lobe epilepsy (TLE) which is a neurological disorder characterised by recurring seizures that originate in the temporal lobe part of the brain. Temporal lobe epilepsy can affect learning in several ways. It can cause difficulties with memory, concentration, and language. Memory problems can cause difficulties with learning new information or remembering previously learned material. Concentration can also be affected, making it difficult to focus and comprehend new topics. Additionally, language can be affected, making it difficult to understand, express, and recall words or concepts. This can become problematic when trying to convert learning and complex ideas or theories into critical thinking. I do want it to be noted that the university and the lecturers I have had have been excellent when dealing with any issues I have had and have offered exemplary levels of support.

My journey into social work began 4 years ago when I was diagnosed with my condition. I remember the doctor advising me that the seizures that I may encounter could be life threatening or could be fatal. The following weeks were difficult for me try to come to terms with this, as every day I had the mindset of "today could be the day". Having worked in kitchens for close to ten years, I came to the realisation that I wanted more out my life and that due to my circumstances I wanted to help people, and social work became an outlet and something to focus on. As I had been out of education for so long, in order for me to get into my desired course, I would have to go through an access course, and this is where I found my disability displaying constraints that affected the way in which I learn.

Initially, things started well, however as we got further into the course, I noticed how I struggled to cope with my studies. This became a problem as the volume of material was getting larger and more complex and I had to read some of material up to ten times before it made any sense. There was more than one occasion that I had no comprehension of what I was supposed to be understanding. In college this wasn't a massive problem for me, we were on campus so there was a physical aspect in the way I interacted with lecturers, also as the class size was under twelve people so I felt more comfortable in airing my trepidations with my lecturers but also to my classmates. I worked hard to get to the stage in which I was just able to start university, furthering my progress to my goal of being a social worker.

I was under no illusions that being at university would be a different ball game and would be extremely difficult, but it was a challenge that I was excited to begin. Then the pandemic hit and lockdown started. After hearing that the course would be conducted completely online prior to starting I didn't give it much thought to be honest. In theory this could be viewed as a good thing as it gave me something to focus on, but it had the adverse effect as I was struggling to comprehend information so became an unhealthy approach when trying to learn the material.

By the time the course started we were already in our own isolated bubbles with lockdown in full effect. Having previous discussions with the disability services before starting about support, who were brilliant, they had devised a learning plan to aide me with my studies. For me it added a totally different dimension on how I was going to be able to participate in the course. For example, I was given a digital voice recorder which I was to use through lectures and then adapt through a programme on my laptop which would correlate what was being said to the PowerPoints given out prior to class. This would give me an audio and visual way of retaining information. For this to happen I would have to ask permission of the lecturer beforehand with it having a less than successful rate. I was told I would need to ask everyone's permission if it would be possible for me to record but that effectively stopped me in my tracks. I didn't have confidence in myself to ask a massive cohort of people that I haven't met if that would be possible. I think this is where my lack of willingness and participation stemmed from. I never really took in the fact that there would be no social aspect in the way in which I would need to learn. I don't know if it would have been different if we were in a live lecture on campus, but the only thing I can draw comparisons from is when I was at college when I felt comfortable talking about my disability in class and being quite honest about when I needed help. In college I had built up strong relationships with the lecturers and my classmates so I think the social aspect was a massive contributor, not only with my confidence but with the acceptance that when I need help, I shouldn't feel embarrassed or guilty about it. So, when this was put into the university stage, I felt isolated during my studies.

It wasn't until my first month that I could see a natural regression, my disability was constraining me in my ability to learn. The university were great at providing equipment and programmes for me to use that would aide my learning but getting deep down into the content which I was learning started to become really difficult to comprehend and understand. Each week we were receiving copious amounts of material to read which I found really difficult to get through, most of which I had to read between four and ten times to have any understanding, and for the most part I never did. This began to take its toll on me as I was always questioning whether or not I was worthy of the opportunity to be at university. This filtered through lectures as they were carried out through zoom. I initially kept my camera on but within the first couple of weeks I would have it switched off in the hope that a lecturer would not ask me a question on the material. I began to experience severe anxiety about being put on the spot and scared to reiterate what I thought the material was. I always had in my mind my fellow classmates judging me - which I must say there was never an instance where this happened, as I had a great set of fellow students and without their help I wouldn't have got to my 3rd year.

As mentioned, there was a social aspect of my university that was completely lacking. This may sound futile but even going through freshers, even going to study in the library, or something minimal like getting a student card I felt like I was missing out on the experience. One thing that had such a positive effect on the way I learned was through our classes WhatsApp group chats. It was really the only time where we as a collective could discuss ideas, but as mentioned I can sometimes have trouble comprehending the material so that highlighted how I was understanding the material. I cannot stress how important those group chats were for me passing each module.

I began to miss classes or have "technical issues" with lecturers who I knew would ask questions regarding material and understanding. As my anxiety grew, I would log out and be angry at myself for not having the confidence to ask if I was right or wrong. This was a debilitating cycle that I ended up in and it's such an unhealthy way in which to learn, but the way in which I battled the feeling of being wrong to ask a lecturer if I was understanding the coursework almost became a natural way to be. It added a totally different dimension on how I was going to be able to participate in the course.

I understand that you are there to learn and questions need to be asked for clarification, but with my disability I had piled so much pressure on my understanding it started to cripple my confidence and at times lost my drive for being on the course. This got me really down and I had some in depth conversations with family and friends about whether I still wanted to do the course, which made me feel like a failure without acknowledging that I do have a disability and although I may have an atypical way of learning that I need to embrace to install confidence in putting myself out there.

For me this was a natural regression. Initially university was something to look forward to, but it slowly became a burden and more a tick box way of doing weekly tasks for each class. We would get videos to watch prior to class using online platforms to learn to me felt like a YouTube way in which to learn. This might have been a preference for some people to learn but it just wasn't for me. It wasn't really a one-size fits all approach but it's what became the new normal and it sort of just stuck. The course did progress where some classes were being recorded which was a massive bonus for me. As I could focus more thoroughly or go over bits that I didn't get in class. This provided me with more in-depth comprehension of the material that I was studying. It wasn't the end of my studying problems but shifted a weight from my shoulders as there was a chance to go through the lectures and to correlate with the reading lists that we were given.

The pandemic and lockdown have had a massive impact on people's lives. It's obviously had a damaging effect on people's health but as it's still a relatively fresh moment in our lifetime, there is still so much research to be done to even comprehend the full effect that it has had on peoples' lives and their mental health. For the purpose of me writing this it had a detrimental effect on my learning process, my capability, and my capacity for comprehension due to my disability.

Writing this has given me great self-reflection into my experience through university, and almost has become a therapeutic outlet for me to discuss and address my story. My journey through social work is far from finished and understand that there is still a lot for me not only to learn but how I adapt to how I learn because of my disability. Through a lack of face-to-face interaction, it created an almost anti-social worker ethos in my studies. This has filtered through on my placement with children and families. I understand that placement is supposed to be challenging but the social aspect was a whole different ball game. On my first day I remember going into the office and seeing an office full of people and the reality of how previously I had the security of sitting on a laptop behind a webcam, it had now all become 'real.' I can only hope that with my experience through lockdown and how I have learned the material will be sufficient enough for me to progress and hopefully qualify.

My Journey

- Karen Rodgers

I have written this article 100 times over in my head. I am a great procrastinator. My mind is always very active, sometimes I think too much. I can be very analytical and a deep reflector, but this brings a positive, particularly for social work, it is an important aspect of practise, right?

My neurodivergent journey started long before my diagnosis of Dyslexia which was late, at the age of 45. As a child, I loved books. They contained knowledge and/or drama, so escapism. Reading them was a vastly different matter though. I really struggled to concentrate and get the words to soak in. I would often skip pages and go to the last few pages, impatient to know the ending, only to then return and skim read the parts I had jumped across. Something that hit me again when I started to study for my Social Work qualification in 2001.

Essay/assignment writing, I would block 5 days for a 2000-word assignment. I would have to shut myself in a room free from distractions, re-read similar perspectives from about six different writers to produce something tangible, a few sentences, a paragraph, that I could then call my own. Painful! I can remember my dissertation taking a few months. Post qualifying and in direct practice, I enjoyed the face-to-face discussions within assessments and reviews. The narrative approach assisted me when inviting people to share their insight into their own lives, their routines, aspects they managed well, enjoyed, and those that were more challenging. Writing up assessments, reviews and reports were my nemesis!

In 2018 I was offered a secondment as a Senior Lecturer in Practice Learning at a local University. I had always been passionate about Social Work Education, having moved out of frontline practice some years earlier. Whilst I had a Post-Grad diploma in Advanced Social Work, I wanted to complete an MA. Ouch, I went straight back to my challenges of reading, writing and poor concentration! An exceptionally long story short (I struggle to write concisely, not surprising I guess!), I went to student support at the university and had a private Dyslexia assessment. It took over 3 hours and I broke down in tears twice. I was being 'assessed' to do what I struggled with, write, 'write about anything for 10 minutes. I lasted about 2 minutes. The next painful part of my 'test' was 'I just want to check your reading speed'! Noooooo! I get distracted, the words do not sink in, I must read, reread, follow with my finger, highlight points. I get bored, skim read and then, not always being aware of what I have done, go back again, so checking my reading speed really was not my favourite part either!

Sadly, that MA is still waiting to be completed, the final bridge that needs crossing, the 'too many words' dissertation. I have the knowledge and experience, but...

Fast forward to the 'almost springtime' of 2023... I am 49. I am perimenopausal, on HRT and struggling. As if my word-finding, pronunciation, short-term memory, reading comprehension, short-term working memory and ability to process information (some aspects of my Dyslexia) were not enough, I have 'brain-fog,' my anxiety moves up and down the scale. I am constantly fatigued, questioning myself and feeling overwhelmed. The next step... finally, just over 3 years after my original diagnosis of Dyslexia I had an 'access to work' assessment. After over 1.5hrs of feeling listened to and understood, it was suggested I followed up with an ADHD assessment. I am at the point of receiving a date, privately, as was informed by my GP the waiting list locally is 2/3 years! The ADHD support groups (which are hidden, or we do not look until we feel we need something) have been invaluable. Watching, listening, and reading (yep, short pieces of text are OK) other people's experiences has provided me with a form of validation. At this point, it is important to say I have not yet been diagnosed and I am not one for putting people in boxes, but carrying out a lot of research, completing numerous screening tools, the box feels comfortable. The diagnosis, I think, would offer validation and more importantly, understanding of the 'why.'

So enough about the 'private' and 'personal' me, 'professional' me has really benefited from the experiential side of my 'neurodivergent journey.' My growing knowledge of Dyslexia and ADHD has been invaluable in my role as an Educator. We talk about 'learning preferences,' how people best like to receive information to support their learning and development. It is also about having insight into some of the challenges, such as 'not meeting timescales,' prioritising, writing-up, seemingly procrastinating, 'not being quick enough' that being neurodivergent can impact on. My eyes are becoming increasingly open to the overlay of complexity, or more concerningly, the discrimination people can and do face – intersectionality.

Racism is very much alive in contemporary Social Work. In March 2022, Social Work England highlighted this deep routed issue when referring to the 'Anti-Racism Report', authored by Gurau and Bacchoo, (2022) which was commissioned by the anti-racism commission group. What can support anti-racist practice for those who are neurodivergent? Tedam's (2011) research looked at black African student's studying Social Work in the UK and raised the importance of taking time to get to know those engaged in learning. The building of trust, becoming aware of similarities and difference can open up further dialogues regarding how culturally, neurodiversity may, or may not be accepted, potentially leading to a person suppressing and/or 'trying' to hide their characteristics. Why am I mentioning this? Because I have seen too many learners from the global majority face additional barriers posed by those involved in assessments questioning levels of 'eye contact,' speed of work, report writing etc.

NICE (2023) state that boys are between 2:1 and 5:1 (as a ratio) more likely to be diagnosed than girls. Elkin (2023) says this is as high as one in nine. NICE (2023) cite the sex difference is down to more 'disruptive behaviour' in boys (linked to associated subtypes) which leads to prompting for assessment referrals. I can remember throwing a chair in primary school once, but clearly did not fit the stereotype! My time has come with the perimenopause, as my oestrogen levels change significantly. This wonderful hormone is required to regulate levels of the brain chemicals like dopamine which do not work as effectively in ADHD. So, everything is dancing to a different tune leaving me seriously out of rhythm!

Being neurodivergent brings many positives and strengths. I am fortunate with my managers that I can be open and honest about how I am feeling. I can get very overwhelmed which leads to periods of time off work, normally a couple of times a year which often fall with the change of seasons (Spring and Autumn). During such times, regular meetup's and support to re-clarifying prioritise really help. For those who are line-managing, please do not see this as a negative, it is about support and a very basic 'reasonable' adjustment.

Talking of 'reasonable adjustments' my Access to Work was a lengthy process, but IT equipment and trickling in, along with some one-to-one support sessions. Building healthy strategies will be invaluable. I used to have too many late nights out of concern 'I had not done enough' in the day. Busy offices are so distracting!

What do I bring to the table? Well as I said at the start, I am a deep 'thinker', I enjoy reflective and creative thinking. My mind is very active, I can normally see multiple perspectives. I am a good listener; I prefer the spoken word rather than written, I will make time for this. I am normally good in a crisis, I do not do drama, rather, look towards solutions that can bring some equilibrium.

References

Elkin, R. (2023) *Women and ADHD: How menopause can affect women with ADHD*. Available at: https://psychiatry-uk.com/women-and-adhd-how-menopause-can-affect-women-with-adhd/. (Accessed 10/04/2023)

Gurau, O. and Bacchoo, A. (2022) *Anti-Racism Report.* Available at: https://www.socialworkengland.org.uk/news/addressing-racism-in-social-work/ (Accessed 09/04/2023)

NICE (2023) *Attention Deficit Hyperactive Disorder. How Common is It?* Available at: https://cks.nice.org.uk/topics/attention-deficit-hyperactivity-disorder/background-information/prevalence/ . (Accessed 10/04/2023)

Tedam, P. (2011). *The MANDELA model of practice learning: An old present in new wrapping?* Journal of Practice Teaching & Learning 11 (2).

When I Was

- Diana Katoto

When I was 7 years old, I remember doing my English and Maths homework on the dining room table with my mum. I hated homework time because I never got any of the answers right. And it really didn't help that I took a long time to get to the wrong answer, this frustrated my mum because she had a limited amount of time on her hands. As a child, I concluded that I was just 'stupid'.

When I was 14 years old, I dreaded when it was my turn to read out loud even though I loved to read. When I read out loud, I was hyperaware of my inability to recognise words or sound them out. This linked to my difficulty with spelling. It was uncomfortable trying to work at the same level as others when I wasn't understanding. When I looked around everyone else was able to read and spell. As a teenager, I concluded that I was 'stupid' but I tried to cover it up with fake confidence so no one would see.

When I was 20 years old, in my first year of university, I received feedback on my assignment and the lecturer had written several detailed paragraphs on the inadequacy of my work. They highlighted the spelling mistakes, grammatical errors, structural problems, and overall flow of the assignment. They gave me the advice to thoroughly proofread my work before submitting it. Unknown to the lecturer, I had proofread my assignment 4 times and was not able to pick up on 90% of the mistakes highlighted. Up until now, I was doing well with faking confidence and pretending I knew what I was doing. I was devastated and somehow concluded that I was 'stuipd'. That 7-year-old child inside of me cried. This experience lead to receiving a diagnosis of Dyslexia and Dyscalculia.

I was never 'stupid' and I shouldn't have been inflicting emotional abuse towards myself. I was a black child in an educational system that allowed me to slip through the net. I look back on my experience and realise that if I was provided with support and strategies earlier, I wouldn't have had to suffer as much. It was also interesting to me that at no point in my education were there any questions from the school or my parents about whether I might have had a learning difficulty. My parents were ignorant regarding learning difficulties and in my culture coming from an African country, it was a taboo subject. It was viewed as a defect of the individual rather than someone just thinking differently. Coming from an immigrant family, I felt the pressure to be academically excellent and any mistakes were viewed as an indication of my lack of intelligence.

To the person reading this, I want you to know that difference doesn't equal failure. You are not 'stupid' or any other word used to bring you down. It's okay if you don't know how to spell or if you struggle with maths. Being neurodivergent isn't a weakness or a fault, and it won't stop you from achieving your goals in life. My personal journey is proof of that. I graduated from university, which was something I never thought I could achieve, and I am working as a social worker. I didn't believe that I could be successful, but I found my own success through accepting myself and my difference.

Reflections of an autistic social worker (who didn't know it at the time)

- *Rose Matthews*

Back in the 1990s, as a social worker, I developed a particular rapport with people who were slipping through the gaps between mental health and learning disability services.

Why was I able to find ways to connect with them? Partly because I adopted a non-traditional approach. Meeting them where they were, getting to know them gently through practical support, and side-by-side sitting, walking, and talking.

I understood why they didn't want to be herded back into day services and preferred to ride the buses all day, or hang out at a local salon, sweeping up hair clippings and drinking tea.

I listened to the songs someone in crisis played on repeat and heard what the lyrics said: "We will survive beyond the grave, and while we sleep, we will be saved."

I liked and respected the people I worked with, recognising that their differences increased the risk of misunderstanding, coercion, and exclusion. I fought their corner when psychiatrists, relatives or neighbours threatened their freedom and rights by trying to force them into services or exclude them from them.

In the last few years, I've realised that the reason I got on so well with my caseload of disengaged 'service users' was because many of them were autistic like me.

I was on their side.

We saw things in a similar way.

We spoke the same kind of language.

We weren't beset by the 'double empathy' problem, so we bonded easily.[1]

If I'd found myself in their position, I'd probably have failed to engage too. Social work practice was supposed to be shifting towards needs-led assessment in the wake of the NHS and Community Care Act (1990), and the introduction of the Care Programme Approach in 1991, but people were still being funnelled into services which happened to be available. When I reflect on my past career as a social worker, I realise that it is inextricably intertwined with policy development.

What had attracted me to social work in the first place was my passion for social justice, and my desire to help people overcome profound inequalities. I wasn't an obvious candidate for a career which depended to such a large extent on interpersonal communication. The fact that I was so painfully shy as a teenager that I became non-speaking in certain situations was a clue about the diagnosis I'd wait 45 years for. But somehow, when it came to advocating for other people, I always seemed to find my voice.

My first job after graduating was in a children's home. I'd been told it was an easy way to begin a career in social work, but this was far from the truth. Some of the children and young people who lived there were being mistreated by other members of staff. I reported my concerns to a senior manager who refused to take any action, so after six months I resigned. When the scandal about abuse in children's homes broke many years later, after I had qualified as a social worker via policing and the probation service, I felt a complicated mixture of emotions. My concerns had been validated but what more could, or should I have done?

People new to care settings, without much formal training, often have great insight into the quality of the care provided but concerns they express tend to be side-lined. Rosemary Thomas, a psychology student on placement at Friern Hospital in the 1960s, described seeing four nurses holding down and force feeding a patient, a patient being 'dragged around' by a nurse, and a nurse 'thumping' a patient. But the investigating committee 'dismissed the student's allegations, describing her as 'an immature, idealistic, young woman.'[2] At Farleigh Hospital in 1968, a newly appointed nurse, Greta Saunders, alleged that patients were being mistreated. The hospital's chief nurse 'thought her an emotional young woman', sacked her and did not investigate the allegations.[3] It takes courage to report abuse, knowing that you risk being gaslighted, victimized, or dismissed.

Mistreatment of people detained in hospitals and secure institutions has continued to the present day. Recent testimony to the government Health and Social Care Committee given by autistic patients and other witnesses highlighted the severity of the abuse and neglect:

> 'Alexis Quinn [...] powerfully described her experiences of being subject to restraint, seclusion and segregation in inpatient hospitals. She told us of being "transported in cages and handcuffs [...] carried like a batter ram", where there were "six to 10 men pinning me to the floor, pulling my pants down, injecting me with sedatives and then secluding me".'[4]

A former in-patient, who was only 16 when she was detained in a mental health unit, described similarly brutal experiences when she was interviewed for a BBC news programme:

> 'They'd restrain me face down on the floor; they're quite aggressive in the way they do it. I was undressed and put in 'safe suits' that were often wet and straight off another patient. Restraints were usually done with six people, I'd say most of them were men. Obviously I was a 16-year-old young woman. It was just humiliating and embarrassing. I was completely naked some of the time. I never even knew what I was being medicated with. They didn't tell me.'[5]

'Care in the community' was supposed to overcome many of the problems associated with large-scale institutional care, but even small domestic-scale settings could become institutions without walls.[6,7] When I began my social work career, I was under no illusions that it was as much about control as care. 'Service users' were expected to eat healthily, budget sensibly, and keep their homes clean and tidy, even though many social workers didn't meet those standards in their own lives. People who found themselves under the supervision of social care staff were often denied basic satisfactions most of us take for granted:

> 'Not only do people strive for freedom in a broad sense, they also enjoy making simple choices, such as whether to engage in unproductive, though harmless, activities, like watching sitcoms on television, eating too many doughnuts, taking the afternoon off from work, or taking a nap before dinner.'[8]

I discovered that all kinds of things were policed, often unofficially. I admired the 'service user' approaching the end of life whose home care worker was trying to stop her smoking by refusing to buy her any tobacco. To get round this she started hiring out her washing machine to neighbours in return for cigarettes. She understood the risks of smoking, but this was the only pleasure she had left. The last time I saw her was on a hot, noisy hospital ward. I was persuaded to go and find a wheelchair so I could take her outside for "one last puff."

When it came to working in people's homes, I had an intuitive understanding of privacy and boundaries. It was obvious to me that the cuddly toys on a chair had been carefully curated not randomly placed there, and that it might cause distress if they were tossed aside carelessly by a visiting Community Psychiatric Nurse who wanted to sit down. Were they not aware of this, or did they not care?

When someone I was working with stopped washing her hair her anti-psychotic medication was about to be increased so I went and asked her why. A lightbulb had blown in a windowless bathroom with an 8-foot-high ceiling. There wasn't any decline in her mental health, just a practical problem that needed fixing. Asking direct questions in an unembarrassed way, rather than making assumptions, was a useful autistic strength.

I often worked with people who struggled to do housework. I understood how quickly chaos can descend into squalor from my own post childbirth depression. There was no judgement from me – just a desire to help them remove barriers to living comfortably by getting adaptations or support. Accepting a cup of tea in such circumstances was often symbolic. Someone I worked with commented that their previous social worker "never sat down, never even took her hands out of her pockets".

Common factors in many of the situations I encountered as a social worker were poverty, precarity, and powerlessness. All too often professionals tried to 'fix' the individual rather than addressing the circumstances which had led to them getting into difficulties in the first place. The autistic (but undiagnosed) people I worked with were at a huge disadvantage when it came to accessing resources. Communication differences, sensory issues, executive functioning challenges, stigma and prejudice were all barriers.

From poor law days onwards there has been an expectation that people will ask for assistance in the 'right way' and show gratitude for it. On 23 September 1947 Mr Peck, a 'chronically ill' man whose family relied heavily on welfare support, wrote deferentially to a charitable organisation:

> 'Do you think I shall be asking too much of you, without any offence whatsoever, as my shoes are not watertight and beyond repair, assist me in obtaining a new pair. I'm sorry to trouble you, at the same time I shall be most pleased if you can. Once again apologising for being such a worry to you, "Size 5" should you require my size in footwear.'[9]

Mr Peck was eventually supplied with a pair of shoes which were slightly too large and had to be worn with thick socks, so they fitted. But when he turned to the charity he had grown to trust after a housing crisis in old age he was informed that he no longer qualified for support. Then, as now, the safety net had holes in it.[7] Granular 'micro histories' like this complement a 'shared typical' approach highlighting the commonality of fear, embarrassment and stigma associated with 'punitive welfare conditionality'.[10]

Social work texts which provided insights 'on being a client' were very powerful during my social work training.[11] Talks by service users and carers also made a deep impression on me and have stayed in my mind. But autistic people without a co-existing learning disability were not represented at all. Autism was subsumed within mental health and learning disability and barely mentioned. When I eventually stumbled across an early edition of Lorna Wing's classic text on the much-misunderstood 'autistic spectrum', I didn't recognise myself in its pages.[12]

During my early adult life, I had developed reasonably convincing neurotypical social skills through watching people, researching human behaviour through psychology, and working in customer facing roles, but it didn't come naturally to me. I struggled to make spontaneous small talk. Inconsequential social conversation was something I found effortful and exhausting. I still do. My social work training gave me a toolbox of techniques based on Motivational Interviewing and Solution Focused Therapy. To my surprise some of them actually worked once I overcame my squeamishness about being manipulative and inauthentic by consciously using them.

'Use of self' was still in vogue when I did my social work training in the 1990s.[13] This might have been a barrier to me applying had I known that I was autistic and internalized the pathologizing notion that autism impairs empathy and the ability to make successful relationships. I didn't regard myself as a 'wounded healer' in a Jungian sense as my early childhood was loving and stable, and my teenage struggles had been attributed to a typically turbulent adolescence. The extent to which I was damaged and disabled by being autistic in an unaccommodating world only became obvious much later. Empathy is something that many social work students seem to struggle with, it is culturally specific and often has to be actively learned and developed.[14] By the time I did my training I already had considerable experience from my personal life, social care, policing, and probation work, which definitely assisted me.

Social work is undeniably relationship based and with hindsight I attribute my preference for relatively clear boundaries to being autistic as well as to 'professional / personal / private' practice considerations.[15,16] We have yet to determine the extent to which Relationship Based Practice in social work is influenced by neurotype, but there is emerging evidence of communication being more successful between matching dyads.[17] Theory and practice have a tricky relationship in the 'swampy lowlands' of social work. Theory often gets retrofitted to justify actions retrospectively rather than being used proactively to assist with sensemaking.[18,19] Emancipatory autistic-authored, critical autism theory is only just beginning to emerge and have an impact.[20]

After qualifying, my social work career evolved in an unconventional way. I managed to get a part-time role in an adult learning disability / mental health team, and I combined this with a PhD. Soon afterwards one of my academic colleagues landed a big research grant, and I was offered a part-time lectureship. I gave up my PhD and started teaching on the social work MA I had just graduated from. Practising and teaching social work 60 miles apart wasn't easy, but I got some invaluable insights by combining these roles.

Any illusions I had about my significance in people's lives as a social worker was soon shattered. Someone I worked with drew an eco-map and put me way out on the margin like a distant planet. I had worried about how they would cope 'out of hours', but then I realised that they were relieved that I didn't visit in the evening or at weekends. That was their private time. Free of scrutiny. Eventually I was forced to choose between these two roles for logistical reasons, and I opted for academia, until the precarity of fixed term contracts got too much for me and I moved back into social services.

I didn't settle anywhere long, I took on new projects, got things sorted out, then moved on, like a Red Adair of the social care world. I moved between research, policy, practice and learning and development roles. I might never have discovered that I was autistic had it not been for the hormonal turbulence of perimenopause pushing me to the point where everything started to unravel.[21] People who knew me through work had no idea how badly things were falling apart at home. After a particularly catastrophic episode, when I was detained in a police cell overnight after what I later realised was an autistic meltdown, I felt compelled to go looking for answers.[22] They were slow in coming. My GP seemed remarkably uncurious about how I had ended up being arrested and what might be done to prevent this from happening in future.

I went through some very difficult times and feared for my safety. I was already a survivor of bereavement by suicide which added to the risk. In the midst of this existential crisis, I got an email out of the blue from a former colleague telling me she'd just had a very late autism diagnosis. We were so similar. That was when I realised I was almost certainly autistic. I had a strong physical reaction. It felt like my heart stopped for a moment and electricity coursed through my body. My face burned. It wasn't that I thought being autistic was a bad thing, it was the glimmer of hope that I might finally have found an answer. I could hardly bear it.

Just before my 59th birthday I managed to find a service skilled in adult autism assessment not too far from where I live. Luckily, I had enough money saved up to bypass my GP and pay for this privately. I simply hadn't got enough energy to persuade him that I was autistic when the fact that I was married with children, and had carved out a fairly successful career, was seen to contradict this.

Finding out that I was autistic didn't fix everything instantly, and like most very late diagnosed people I mostly had to fend for myself. But uncovering who I was, through a painstaking process of unpicking the past was a vital step in recovering myself. It also opened the possibility of connecting with other people who experience the world like I do. New insights emerge as we share our stories and discover aspects of our lives reflected in each other's.

My autism diagnosis was a life-changing, watershed moment, a pivotal point around which my whole life turned. With hindsight I can see plainly why things unfolded as they did. It had always been obvious that I was autistic – how could this have been missed by countless teachers, GPs, and counsellors? My diagnosis came so late that I had more life behind me than ahead of me. I knew I needed help but where to find it? The 'Improving Access to Psychological Therapies' (IAPT) team told me they were "not allowed to refuse me a service" but made it clear they couldn't really help me because I was autistic. They referred me on to the Community Mental Health Team (CMHT).

I had several disastrous meetings with an Assistant Psychologist at the CMHT which always began "so how are things?" followed by an unstructured, meandering conversation. I got my partner to accompany me to an appointment to help me find out why I hadn't had a proper assessment. It turned out that a formulation and care plan had already been drafted without any input from me. I asked for copies and after a long delay was given them. I could scarcely believe what I read. Somehow, I had acquired a different family structure and a diagnosis of EUPD (Emotionally Unstable Personality Disorder). I was literally speechless and overwhelmed, so we went and sat in the car. I knew from my social work experience how badly people are treated when they carry such a 'dangerous' label. I was full of fear and dread.

When I challenged the formulation, I was told that there had been an "administrative error". It looked to me as if someone else's document could have been used as a template, and clumsily over-typed, leaving 'EUPD' and some of their family history undeleted. Records are not boring; recording matters.[23,24] I'm still not entirely convinced that this was an administrative mistake. The rapid back tracking may also have had something to do with me telling them I was a former social worker. I spoke at length with commissioners about my experiences and sent them a written statement. Tragically, other people treated by the same mental health trust didn't survive being misdiagnosed with a Borderline Personality Disorder.[25]

After that initial iatrogenically harmful attempt to get mental health support I started using a formal advocacy service and was eventually allocated a social worker. We bonded in despair over the recent general election. The social worker told me he had cried when he heard the result because of the impact it would have on the people he worked with. I had cried too. I felt safe and confident working with him, but when Covid struck shortly afterwards I discharged myself, knowing that an already overstretched service would soon be overwhelmed.

During the pandemic I watched an interview with an Irish autistic therapist on YouTube. He spoke very movingly about his connection with the natural world, and I knew instinctively that he would be able to help me. We had sessions on Zoom. He encouraged me to recognise that it was likely to take me quite a long time to adjust to being autistic. Whenever I feel as if I should have made more progress, I compare the years

I've lived with and without this knowledge. The current ratio is 58:4, which puts things into perspective. Even now, more than four years on, it's still 'early days'.

I haven't been registered as a social worker since 2012, but it's still an important part of my identity, influencing how I see myself, and how I relate to the world. I have become an autistic autism researcher, exploring autistic people's experiences of menopause; relationships and sexuality; retirement; death and dying. Until recently I also worked part-time in a prison, where there were many neurodivergent people, mostly unrecognised. But these days, when it comes to toxic environments I am like a canary in a mine. Empathic distress, having to camouflage aspects of my identity, and the hostile sensory environment made it impossible for me to continue.

Sadly, most autistic people over the age of 40 (and many younger ones too) still don't have a clue about their neuro-identity. It would be easy enough to find them, or provide information to help them identify themselves, but no one seems to care much about the recognition of autism later in life apart from those of us who are neurodivergent. Only we know the devastating consequences of not realising that we are autistic, and the profound benefits of discovering who we really are.

Autistic people are disproportionately represented in homeless populations. It's easy to see how a perfect storm of precarious employment, poor health, poverty, and limited or non-existent support networks can result in homelessness.[26] Many late diagnosed autistic people live life on the edge and the demographic profile of the population means the crisis of older autistic people lacking appropriate support is happening now (our problems don't conveniently hold off until we've been recognised).

> "The assumption that we must have worked it out by now if we're still walking, talking and have a pulse can hide a grim reality of difficult, isolated and unfulfilled lives. Over time I've learned the hard way how to present well in public but behind closed doors it's a different matter. I live in a house where the lights, fridge, cooker and washing machine have packed up one by one but I lack the skills to sort it out, and I'd rather live in darkness than have someone I don't know in my personal space. I may be a graduate with a high IQ but I struggle financially due to a lifetime of subsisting on a single, small part-time income. I lack close family or friends to support me and on the many days I spend alone I am liable to forget how to talk. Sometimes someone just giving me a reality check of the "have you eaten today?" kind would be useful."[27]

When it comes to residential or day care services in older age the thought of being parked in a vinyl chair on the perimeter of a noisy day-room with staff jollying me along fills me with horror. My senses would be assaulted, I'd be in a constant state of shutdown or meltdown. I worked somewhere like that once, where an elderly retired professor kept disappearing during the entertainment. We'd find him sitting at a desk in an empty office looking perfectly at home. I would rather become a 21st century 'Lady in the Van', or seek sanctuary in 'Nomadland', than subject myself to the privations of a forced social environment.[28,29,30]

My desire for change has always come with a large 'side' of politics. For me social work is as much about addressing the structural as the personal. The perspective I see things from is distinctly 'biopsychosocioeconomic'. Perhaps it is partly the profound impact that my environment has on me that makes me adopt this position. I can only see things from an ecological perspective – nothing else makes sense.

Every day since my autism discovery has brought new insights. I'm still reinterpreting past events and probably always will be. I've adopted a more radical approach to self-care, avoiding toxic situations, and removing myself as quickly as possible if I accidentally stumble into them. I don't always pick up on interoceptive signals and get the message that I am hungry, tired or thirsty, so I try to anticipate my needs, and factor in ways of reminding myself. I try to keep enough energy in reserve to cope with unexpected demands, and schedule in recovery time after enjoyable or stressful events that I know will be exhausting.

Life has its challenges - concerns about global inequality, climate change, the cost-of-living crisis, and the demise of democracy loom large - but even so I'm embracing old age with a new-found sense of confidence, self-acceptance, and joy. Social media connects me with people who experience the world the same way as I do. Yesterday I cried tears of happiness and relief as someone I know through Twitter got their autism diagnosis. Connectedness with other autistic people runs deep, even though we are diverse, multi-cultural, intersectional, individual, and unique.

References

1. Milton, D., Gurbuz, E. and Lopez, B. The "double empathy problem": Ten years on. *Autism*. 2022;26(8):1901-1903. doi:https://doi.org/10.1177/13623613221129123

2. Hilton, C. Improving Psychiatric Care for Older People. Springer International Publishing; 2017. doi:https://doi.org/10.1007/978-3-319-54813-5

3. Hilton, C. A Tale of Two Inquiries: Sans Everything and Ely. *The Political Quarterly*. 2019;90(2):185-193. doi:https://doi.org/10.1111/1467-923x.12692

4. The treatment of autistic people and people with learning disabilities - Health and Social Care Committee - House of Commons. publications.parliament.uk. https://publications.parliament.uk/pa/cm5802/cmselect/cmhealth/21/2102.htm

5. Former West Lane Hospital patient recalls "humiliating" treatment. BBC News. https://www.bbc.co.uk/news/uk-england-tees-48869472. Published July 4, 2019. Accessed February 26, 2023.

6. Bartlett, P. and Wright, D. Outside the Walls of the Asylum : On "Care and Community" in Modern Britain and Ireland. Athlone Press; 1999.

7. Walmsley, J. and Rolph, S. The development of community care for people with learning difficulties 1913 to 1946. Critical Social Policy. 2001;21(1):59-80. doi:https://doi.org/10.1177/026101830102100102

8. Bannerman, DJ., Sheldon, JB., Sherman, JA. and Harchik, AE. Balancing the Right to Habilitation with the Right to Personal Liberties: The Rights of People with Developmental Disabilities to Eat Too Many Doughnuts and Take a Nap. Journal of Applied Behavior Analysis. 1990;23(1):79-89. doi:https://doi.org/10.1901/jaba.1990.23-79

9. Edwards, R. and Gillies, V. Insights from the Historical Lived Experience of a Fragmented Economy of Welfare in Britain: Poverty, Precarity and the Peck Family 1928–1950. Genealogy. 2020;4(1):20. doi:https://doi.org/10.3390/genealogy4010020

10. McIntosh, I. and Wright, S. Exploring what the Notion of "Lived Experience" Offers for Social Policy Analysis. Journal of Social Policy. 2018;48(03):449-467. doi:https://doi.org/10.1017/s0047279418000570 (cited in 9.)

11. Howe, D. *On Being a Client: Understanding the Process of Counselling and Psychotherapy*. SAGE, 1993.

12. Wing, L. The Autistic Spectrum: A Guide for Parents and Professionals. United Kingdom, Constable, 1996.

13. Gordon, J. and Dunworth, M. The fall and rise of "use of self"? An exploration of the positioning of use of self in social work education. *Social Work Education*. 2016;36(5):591-603. doi:https://doi.org/10.1080/02615479.2016.1267722

14. Gair, S. Social Work Students' Thoughts on Their (in)Ability to Empathise with a Birth Mother's Story: Pondering the Need for a Deeper Focus on Empathy. Adoption & Fostering. 2010;34(4):39-49. doi:https://doi.org/10.1177/030857591003400405

15. Ingram, R. and Smith, M. Relationship-based practice: emergent themes in social work literature. Iriss. Published November 6, 2018. https://www.iriss.org.uk/resources/insights/relationship-based-practice-emergent-themes-social-work-literature

16. Roesch-Marsh, A. Reflecting on boundaries and the use of self in professional relationships: insights from social pedagogy. Families, Relationships and Societies. 2019;8(2):345-349. doi:https://doi.org/10.1332/204674319x15583479932873

17. Crompton, CJ., Ropar, D., Evans-Williams, CV., Flynn, EG. and Fletcher-Watson, S. Autistic peer-to-peer information transfer is highly effective. Autism. 2020;24(7):1704-1712. doi:https://doi.org/10.1177/1362361320919286

18. Schön, DA. The Reflective Practitioner: How Professionals Think in Action. Basic Books; 1983.

19. Rycroft, P. When theory abandons us - wading through the "swampy lowlands" of practice. Journal of Family Therapy. 2004;26(3):245-259. doi:https://doi.org/10.1111/j.1467-6427.2004.00281.x

20. Botha, M., Dibb, B. and Frost, DM. "Autism is me": an investigation of how autistic individuals make sense of autism and stigma. Disability & Society. 2020;37(3):1-27. doi:https://doi.org/10.1080/09687599.2020.1822782

21. Moseley, RL., Druce, T. and Turner-Cobb, JM. "When my autism broke": A qualitative study spotlighting autistic voices on menopause. Autism. 2020;24(6):1423-1437. doi:https://doi.org/10.1177/1362361319901184

22. Matthews, R. The Night I Lost My Freedom, and Got It Back Again. Autism in Adulthood. 2022;4(1):1-2. doi:https://doi.org/10.1089/aut.2021.0093

23. Prince, K. Boring Records? : Communication, Speech, and Writing in Social Work. Jessica Kingsley Publishers, 1996.

24. O'Keefe, R., Maclean, S. Case Recording in Social Work with Children and Families. Kirwin Maclean Associates, 2023.

25. Langley, L. and Price, E. Death by a Thousand Cuts: Report into the Tees, Esk and Wear Valleys NHS Foundation Trust "BPD+" Protocol. Accessed February 27, 2023. https://www.researchgate.net/publication/360939741_Death_By_A_Thousand_Cuts_Report_into_the_Tees_Esk_and_Wear_Valleys_NHS_Foundation_Trust_BPD_Protocol http://dx.doi.org/10.13140/RG.2.2.34275.02085

26. Stone, B., Cameron, A. and Dowling, S. The autistic experience of homelessness: Implications from a narrative enquiry. Autism. Published online June 25, 2022:136236132211050. doi:https://doi.org/10.1177/13623613221105091

27. Dunne, S. Autism as an adult: "On the many days I spend alone I forget how to talk." the Guardian. Published September 16, 2015. https://www.theguardian.com/social-care-network/social-life-blog/2015/sep/16/autism-as-an-adult-on-the-many-days-i-spend-alone-i-forget-how-to-talk

28. Oró-Piqueras, M. and Casado-Gual, N. Exploring Care Through Alan Bennett's The Lady in the Van: Extending Meanings, Encountering Otherness. de Medeiros K, ed. The Gerontologist. 2020;60(7):1254-1260. doi:https://doi.org/10.1093/geront/gnaa024

29. McQuillan, C. Home is a question mark. The Lancet Psychiatry. 2021;8(12):1042. doi:https://doi.org/10.1016/s2215-0366(21)00445-4

30. Joyes, EC., Jordan, M., Winship, G. and Crawford, P. Inpatient Institutional Care: The Forced Social Environment. Frontiers in Psychology. 2021;12. doi:https://doi.org/10.3389/fpsyg.2021.690384

My Dyslexia Journey and Beyond

- Mark Stockley-Haylock

I look back to my early childhood with a few vivid images relating to my Dyslexia diagnosis, that lead me on a path into my teens, and into adulthood of nothing but struggles and misunderstanding, but now I feel that path is corrected, and I can see the light.

It all started at primary school, I was around 5 years old and as I was learning to write, I was writing in mirror writing. Being young I did not really understand what was happening, only that my parents were taking me to the Dyslexic institute in Newcastle. I remember being in the room without my parents and there being a man in the room, I can't remember specifics about him, but I do remember it being a large room, with high ceiling with a wooden large table, and being it being very cold in there while I took part in the tests. These tests ranged from arranging shapes to reading and writing.

I don't remember much of what happened next, as I transitioned from mainstream school to private school at the age of 6. Looking back now, I can see how difficult this was, and the challenges I faced making new friends there, but I did, and still speak to a few of them to this day. My first teacher was lovely, she felt like a second mum. My first year at private school, was the first time I had experienced exams... or as I wrote it 'eggsams'. I remember not doing particularly well, but I was young, so what's the problem right? I do remember one thing about that classroom, the teacher making notes on the board about everyone in the class, positive things we had done, words of encouragement, and I remember mine reading words to the effect of "I wish everyone's handwriting would improve as much as Mark's." This was one of the few times I had achieved something positive, even just improving my handwriting.

It took a further year before I recall anything significant. This was when I remember seeing the letter from the Dyslexic Institute. I don't recall the contents, but I remember the logo being part of a face drawn in thick pencil or crayon. I was being taken to an optician to be fitted for tinted glassed. Apparently, this would help me with my reading. I remember testing both blue and yellow and orange lenses and feeling that the yellow benefited me more. It would be a couple of weeks before these would be ready to collect. Looking back, I don't recall how I felt, but I do remember expecting to be able to read better and with more confidence.

My glasses arrived, and I remember picking them up with my mum in Durham City. They were in a brown faux crocodile skin case. I tried them on in the opticians to ensure they fitted, and my mum bought me one of those strings that fits to the back to wear around my neck.

I went into school the next day, nervous, but ready to wear them and try them out in the real world. What happened next was a only a small exchange, but even now when I look back on it, I can still feel the embarrassment and anxiety.

My teacher in my second year was an older man, very old in fact with an "old school" attitude. Someone you might imagine you would see from the book "Tom Brown's School Days". This is not to say it made him a "bad" teacher, but certainly challenging.

The morning came to go to school, I had my briefcase which contained my books and pencil case and now a glasses case. We had been to assembly and roll call as normal, and I remember sitting down in the morning lesson. The classroom was in a new part of the school, fairly modern for the time, decently sized and the classic school tables which seat two people. Being left handed I always (when I could) sat on the left side as not to bump elbows with my classmate. I don't specifically remember what lesson it was, but it feels like it was R.E. or "scripture" as he liked to call it. Taking out my books and pencil case, no problem, then taking out the glasses case, I could feel myself getting a little nervous. I opened the case, took them out and put them on. I closed the case with a snap. It only took moments for him to spot me. "Take those sunglasses off" he bellowed. I could feel everyone in the class looking at me. I took them off and hid them away in my briefcase. I felt ashamed.

I remember my mum asking how I was getting on with the new glasses... "great" I'd tell her. I was too ashamed to wear them at school, and too worried my mum would be upset I wasn't wearing them. This was my life now. I struggled on in silence, ashamed and afraid to speak up about anything. My confidence was gone. I was no longer putting my hand up to answer questions or taking part in things.

I struggled keeping focus in lessons, often being distracted by the smallest of things. I even remember one time in Latin, our teacher was talking and I could hear everything going on around me, slowly his talking turned into noise, as I look down and find myself colouring in my fingernails with a highlighter, I can still hear "white noise," totally zoning out... I glance up and see him kneeling in front of my desk looking at him, smiling, and everyone in the class laughing. How long had he been there? A few seconds? A few minutes? Who knows. But this was not an isolated incident of distraction or lack of focus. Looking back this now feels like a slippery slope.

I started to get into sports and really started to excel at it. I had a new focus in my life. I was good at rugby, and I wasn't a bad runner either. Had it not been for sports, I am not sure how I would have fared.

At 13 we moved to "big school." Unfortunately, that summer I lost my father to a brain tumour. I was due to go to Barnard Castle School, but due to the trauma, it was felt best that perhaps I stayed closer to home, and be around friends, so arrangements were made for me to attend Durham School.

I thrived at this school... athletically. By this point my Dyslexia had been swept under the carpet and I was just cracking on with school. I was in the bottom set for everything, except maths. I really enjoyed maths. I liked its logic and patterns. It made sense to me. I had a great rugby season, and great athletics season in the summer.

GCSE's were not far away, and my mum contacted the school about my Dyslexia and I was given extra time during exams. But that was all the support I was offered or given. I didn't do particularly well. But that's just me, I simply was not very good academically. Things didn't click. I couldn't concentrate in lessons. I could write great stuff, just not nail the answer. C'est la vie.

Due to my poor grades, I had to have a meeting with the headmaster before starting my A-Levels, luckily I was given a lifeline and I was allowed to stay on. I had the same issues of drifting off and generally struggling in lessons.

Had it not been for my sporting achievements, I am not sure where I would have fit in socially. There are groups in mainstream schools, and we were no different. I tried to be friends with everyone as much as I could, but my rugby lead me down a path with the "cool" group. I was still a peripheral figure, liked enough to be part of the group, but not heavily involved enough to be "top dog." Saturday nights down Durham at Klute are nights I won't forget, but school life is something I can put behind me.

I moved into higher education with the idea that I wanted to be a solicitor. A tall order, all things considered, and managed my first year at university studying my LLB. I met someone at university, Dave (of course everyone knows a Dave), he was really into his computer games, something which I had never really put much thought into, other then playing the likes of Super Mario Kart on the Super Nintendo. But he encouraged me to get a PC and play online games with him. He was great, he was from the area and knew some great places to go for a "liquid lunch."

However, university life was not for me, I was either not ready for higher education or I was ready to just move on in life and get on, or perhaps both. It took a lot for me to tell my mum I was done, and I wanted to leave as I know how proud she was of me for going to university and desperately wanted me to get a degree. But it was not to be.

I was still in touch with Dave, however I did not play PC games with him anymore, as I made friends with someone else on the game we played. I played a lot. Hours every day. Hiding behind my online character "Stockcube." Not needing to hear my voice or see me. It was all written in text chat, long before the days online voice chat was popularised. I was hooked. I was focused.

I got my first job working in admin at a prison, working on the drug rehab wing. This felt like a baptism of fire, there was lot to take in and lots to consider, but I did very much enjoy things. I had a focus and clear aims in life. Dyslexia was well and truly in the back seat, it was just something that was there which effected my day-to-day life, but I dealt with it. It was hidden, and why would I need to tell people?

By the end of 2004 I had secured a job with Durham Constabulary and served 4 years 363 days... but who's counting? Looking back at my time, so many aspects of my role I was able to really focus and "get stuck in," distraction wasn't an issue. My writing wasn't an issue. But seemingly something was, and I was not happy. I was performing well, but I knew this road would come to an end.

But, this "gaming" thing I had picked up, I was in deep. I met someone called Paul, from down south. We played together for hours and hours, everything around just seemed to disappear, like I had blinkers on... like my Latin lesson some 12 years prior.

At this point, my now wife (girlfriend at the time) used to joke about me making loud noises, whistling or clapping. I laughed it off as it was me just being an idiot. She was adamant there was more to me than just my Dyslexia. But I shrugged it off and denied it, and said I'm fully aware I'm doing, but I just need to release.

She had become accustomed my gaming, after all, I was gaming when we met, she knew it was my "hobby." Our daughter Sophie was born in 2012, and by this time I had been playing World of Warcraft for around 7 years. My life was on a bit of downer, I had been back to college to obtain my 'Preparing to Teach in the Lifelong Learning Sector' qualification, with a view of teaching adults key skills seeking employment, however this did not pan out how I wanted and found myself in an endless circle. I was working in retail, just enough to keep us going, but never able to push myself. My focus lay with my gaming. Once I put that headset on nothing else mattered. Everything around my closed down, and it was just me and the screen.

I needed something else, I needed to reset. So I started my law degree again, part time with the Open University. This was difficult, it was self-driven and it was hard to get focused and "in the zone." I worked hard and managed to get my modules for my level 4 done over 2 years, but I was spent. It was exhausting, mentally.

I managed to secure a job working in sales. It was only a few minutes away from home and the hours suited childcare. I won't say much about this, other than it was a miserable time working for a bully. 4 ½ years, felt like a jail sentence.

Sophie was getting older, and words which haunt me to this day "daddy you're spending too much time on the computer." It was those words in February 2019, which pushed my retirement from World of Warcraft. I had been playing since 2005. I had met fantastic people, met up with some in Lincoln and Nottingham. That May would be a final meet up, and retirement party for myself and my online friends. 12 of us in total managed to make it, with some coming from Sweden and The Netherlands.

I didn't really have many friends "in real life," living my life online was all I had. I was fed up in my job and my wife knew it. She was already in her first year of her social work degree and loving it. She encouraged me to apply, I wasn't sure, was it for me? Could I handle studying and doing assignments? I'd struggle with my Dyslexia and being able to focus right?

I applied in December 2019, and had my interview in January 2020. Three days later I was accepted onto the course.

However, I am not telling my bully of a boss. I am leaving it until I only need to give my 2 weeks' notice.

Then we have lockdown 2020. This was a blessing in disguise. It gave me time away from work to refresh and renew. All 3 of us were at home together. Enjoying each other's company. We regularly look back on this as a good time in our lives considering everything that was going on around us.

September 2020, and I hand my notice in. People say, "that's a weight off my shoulders," to use this phrase would be an understatement. All the stress of him blowing his top every time I made a small mistake was gone. The anxiety of waking up in the morning and feeling sick at the thought of going into work... gone. I didn't tell him I was Dyslexic, as I knew he would use it against me in some way, previously I felt trapped, now I was free. I had something new to look forward to.

Everything was in place for me to start, student loan – sorted, new bag – sorted, new pencil case and pens – sorted, and a new set of fancy notebooks – sorted. I was really excited to get going with this. For the first time in a very long time, I felt like I had something positive to look forward to. My first day, I sat at the front of the class. The tables were still separated as there were still some Covid restrictions in place, but to my left was Christina and to my right was Andy.

One of my first interactions with Andy was "Mark have you got ADHD?" Andy was great, he has ADHD, and we have built a great friendship over these 3 years, especially our "liquid lunch" at the Marquis of Granby in Durham, I think they were serving rocket fuel that afternoon. Andy noticed things in my behaviour, I was aware of these things, and even my wife was aware of, but he almost validated them. Every time he would pick up on something, "Mark I think you've got ADHD." With a simple reply of "nah don't be daft man Andy." Numerous times over level 4 and 5 he would say something, but I never took enough notice of him.

It wasn't until the summer of 2022 when things started falling into place. Andy's persistence, along with things I had been reading about as well as comments my wife had made in passing made me look into things more. I was in the middle of researching something for my dissertation, specifically the Idiots Act 1886. Something popped in my head... "who was the King or Queen back then?" That now was the most important thing in the world to me (it was Queen Victoria if you wanted to know). But this path led me down a rabbit hole of research... specifically Belgium and how it became the Belgium we know today going back to the Dutch revolution. Why? I have no idea, but what a wild ride that was. Then suddenly like someone flicked a switch in my brain... I think to myself "Mark, what are you doing?" and nearly 2 hours have passed and the Idiots Act 1884 seems like a distant memory.

I get in touch with Andy to chat about this, and to seek advice, we chat for some time, I tell him what happened, and explain that in lessons, despite how interesting it can be, sometimes the lecturers voice just turns to noise, almost white noise, and I might be sat looking at them, as though I am listening and taking it all in, but it's just noise I hear, while my head is doing other things "are those chicken burgers still in the freezer? Who are Newcastle playing at the weekend? I wish someone would open the window it's warm in here. I wonder what dogs hear when we speak." He orders to me research more and watch some YouTube vloggers with ADHD.

So many things from my childhood fit into place now, listening to peoples struggles become so relatable, aspects of what I now know as 'hyperfocus' have given me an understanding of what I just put down to Dyslexia and being thick. I am starting to get an understanding of my own behaviour and my own self-worth.

I ask Andy what I need to do to get an assessment. I get my GP appointment and referral submitted, and a short time later I get my initial assessment appointment.

For the first time, I am not nervous, I am excited. Do I have ADHD? Is this the answer I have been looking for?

The assessment lasted for just over an hour and half, we chatted about all sorts of things, she even knew one of the lecturers on my Social Work course, I felt relaxed and comfortable. We spoke about everything I have mentioned above and more. At the end the clinician, couldn't formally diagnose ADHD, but explained that normally there is a meeting at the end of the day to discuss cases and how next to action them, which of course I understood. However, she said that she didn't feel it was necessary with me, as in her opinion it was evident that I have ADHD, and in her words a "smidge" of Autism.

As of writing, that was only just over a week ago. I have never felt so relaxed about myself, now that I am on this road, I feel it is bright and I can see clearly. I am getting an understanding of myself and why I am the way I am. My emotions, the way I act and feel, the things I say.

The journey is only just beginning for me, and even at 40 years old, I feel I have the whole world at my feet. I not longer feel ashamed or embarrassed about hidden disabilities I may have, but I feel enabled and have direction. I wish I could tell my 7 year old self that it will be OK in the end.

Bona Fide: neither specious nor counterfeit...more often sincere than genuine, yet always 'in good faith'...

- *Aga M. Buckley, Alice, Cat & the Mad Hatter.*

Let's begin with a little word puzzle...I admit I needed to check what specious (adjective) means. In case you are wondering, according to the Merriam-Webster online dictionary, specious refers to "having a false look of truth or genuineness". Forgive me for this diversion, as I have a rationale for choosing **Bona Fide** as a starting term in the title. Unintended consequences of using interesting words manifest themselves in unplanned aspiration of 'linguistic analytics' of other exciting terms that grab my attention... at times forgetting where I started to begin with... Still, **Bona Fide** was chosen for its primary meaning: **'being actually and exactly what is claimed'** (Merriam-Webster, 2022). The title already suggests my, perhaps, a little clumsy take on characteristics portrayed as essential in the social work profession. I use synonyms of **Bona Fide** to play with the nuance of 'genuine authenticity', considering (neuro) differences and their intersections in the context of social work professional (and personal) identity. I use (neuro) in brackets, hoping to reach beyond the synapses between neurons in our brains, acknowledging the uniqueness of said identity beyond human physiology.

This is a story, a tale perhaps... for reflection might sound overly ambitious, in which I attempt to introduce an alternative side, look or image of a Social Worker. And suppose you noted the authors, including characters from "Alice in Wonderland". In that case, I credit those I cannot name, appreciating their impact on the **'image' of a Social Worker** I propose here.

This 'image' is mine and yet not mine at all.

I wonder about things you see. Never sure if you see 'stubborn and rigid' or 'tenacious and adaptable', uncomfortably 'full on' or 'passionate', perhaps utterly 'inappropriate' and far from simply 'honest'. Blaming cultural differences for things I do not always get, possibly getting them later than I wished... cringing in embarrassment for being overly British in all my non-Britishness. Feeling defeated in the quest for acting 'normal' with the jokes or small talk mastered to the point, I have no idea when to stop... Yes, I can talk about the weather for an excessively long time... how British of me!

With so many aspects of fitting into a social and professional norm, when I peel the layer of cultural or mere language variations, I quickly stumble onto the next one, and the one after... and one more, much depending on who I am, or expected to be, in the context. Although apparently equitable, somehow, each layer quietly looks away from the discomfort of difference, often insisting on uniform sameness.

As a Social Worker, I worry about social work when it fails to recognise professionalism in the richness of interpretations, perceptions, and understandings. There might be resignation, or could it be the comfort (?) of relying ever so confidently on frameworks, statements, and procedures... far too frequently excused from ever questioning their relevance to the Person they are supposed to serve. I fear social work risks becoming a discipline and practice of 'enabling' a better fit into a social norm rather than one that truly sees and argues for the value of... dare I say... 'misfit'.

As you see, I tend to go on a tangent, which is part of the 'image', I'm afraid... It gets significantly worse when I feel strongly about something. To make matters a little more complicated, I think and feel a lot, most of the time... and fast, and not only because I am a Social Worker. These are the times I am genuinely me, and it takes much effort and practices to curb the enthusiasm to appear thinking and feeling 'less'. The Mad Hatter in Tim Burton's (2010) movie "Alice in Wonderland" describes it as a 'muchness'. One might say it is a gift... others see a curse. Perhaps it is two in one. Naturally, I long to remain "much more muchier", using Mad Hatter's terminology from the movie when he complains about Alice losing her 'muchness'. You see, it is a desirable quality in Wonderland, as according to the Cat, everyone there is mad (Carroll, 2012). Experience tells me the same 'muchness' appears less welcomed in our societal realm, not to mention the professional sphere of social work. Hence, one's genuineness can no longer remain genuine, altered by demanded effort to meet the expected 'norm'.

As I return from Wonderland, I ponder the frequency of one person 'fitting' another into a category, making sure the 'correct' boxes are ticked. Indeed, a well-meant approach meets an organisational flaw with a computer system allowing one and only one box per person, so it is left unquestioned. As we consider so-called 'very basic' demographic data, everyone seems to collect with much disregard for its sensitive nature; asking why someone needs it or how (and whom) it serves remains problematic. Uncertainty strikes if there is no box to tick. This is quickly followed by a sigh of relief at the sign of the 'Other' box available. And it becomes a custom not to acknowledge the identity one recognises for themselves, as the 'Other' serves its purpose of containing the 'misfit'... without 'othering' those who do not fit... of course.

And so, we rely on boxes to justify allocating resources, assess risk, or recommend others to expand the same repertoire of boxes and assign a suitable label. We do that, knowing that such a label inevitably attracts the stigma and skewed conclusion about who the Person is. Yes, that same label that most likely guarantees or at least brings closer, some form of help. Most of us recognise the power of labels, their potential for validation and acceptance, and the cruelty of judgement and exclusion. I wonder if this explains our 'label immunity' within the profession. More so, whether energy invested in working with people we serve should ever justify or distract from the very limitations and gaps in attitudes we face from each other in that respect.

Having humbling teachers in people I worked with over the years, most of whom labelled and categorised before they even started a conversation on what they wanted or needed, I never stop asking myself what differentiates 'normal' from 'mad'. And while I am resigned to seeing there is a box for everyone... naively perhaps, I fantasise about being 'box-free' with people, acknowledging the essential validity of natural differences within humankind and as many versions of 'normal' as there are.

I promised an 'image' of a Social Worker at the start. While I am hesitant to insist on Bona Fide adding to my story, this might as well be my way of showing what the longing for added complexity looks like... where things could be so straightforward. I see the rigid temptation to use detail that matters or means something to me to compensate...

'in good faith'...for things I overlook as they skip my attention.

And so, the tale ends with something very dear to me.

It is mine, as it was gifted to me by someone who cared enough to take the time to 'imagine and think' it for and of me.

It is mine as this is me, skilfully crafted when we met for the last time to say goodbye.

It is me, as seen by someone who stayed where they were in their journey while I changed my direction.

To credit people I worked with and learned from over the years, I borrow Alices' response to Mad Hatter, asking if he has gone mad (Burton, 2010). Alice says:

"I'm afraid so. You're entirely bonkers. But I'll tell you a secret... all the best people are."

...and I sincerely believe this is not only the case in Wonderland.

Aga M. Buckley (2022) digital image of an original hand-drawn portrait produced by a person she worked with for several years while in front-line mental health social work practice, received as a parting, thank-you gift.

References:

Burton, T. (2010) Alice in Wonderland. United States of America: Walt Disney Pictures, Walt Disney Studios Motion Pictures.

Carroll, L. (2012) ALICES ADVENTURE IN WONDERLAND. London, England: National Trust Books.

Merriam-Webster Dictionary (2022), 'Bona fide definition & meaning'. Available at: https://www.merriam-webster.com/dictionary/bona%20fide (Accessed: 10 November 2022).

English as an Additional Language or Neurodiverse?

- Kulchuma Begum

Before delving into my experiences as a neurodiverse social worker let's familiarise ourselves with what English as an Additional Language (often referred to as EAL) is. According to the Department of Education a pupil is recorded as using EAL if "they are exposed to a language at home that is known or believed to be other than English" and will be recorded as such throughout their education and life if they have been identified as EAL when they start school at the age of 3-5 years old (The Bell Foundation, 2023).

I immigrated to live in the UK at the age of four with zero knowledge of the English language or culture. I had to start from scratch and was supported in my education as a student with EAL. I cannot recall the early days of primary school, but I remember when I was preparing for my SATs in year six I was given extra support to help with my reading and comprehension this continued into year seven of high school as I was in the lower sets, but as I made progress and moved up a set this was stopped. I remember struggling throughout my education and having to work harder to get the grades my peers and friends achieved with little to no effort and putting this down to just being a bit dumb. Having said all this, I was fortunate enough to leave secondary school with GCSEs at grade C for English and Science but needing to re-sit my Maths. When I started further education at college it was the same story, struggling to understand the work, having to put in the extra hours and not being able to achieve the desired grades, but I did manage to pass my Maths.

Coming from a family that did not understand the importance of education due to not being educated themselves and my older siblings only studying to GCSE level I also gave up on further education for a mixture of reasons but the main one being I wasn't bright enough and therefore would amount to nothing. Having given up on any aspirations I completed my NVQ level 3 in childcare and worked as a nursery nurse then teaching assistant and remained working with children in various settings for the next 16 years. Due to the lack of education I struggled to progress in any careers and found that I had got stuck in a rut. I was unsuccessfully applying for jobs and during feedback from the interviews the reasons given for not being appointed were due to having other candidates that had a higher qualification than me. Having talked about this with my husband I was encouraged to pursue education again, when I explained that I had never been academic and did not think this would be a possibility he pointed out that I was capable of more and was possibly held back due to my lack in confidence.

Having taken some time off work due to ill health I bit the bullet and applied for university to study social work. I attended the open days, asked all the important questions about being a mature student and dug out all my qualifications then sent off my application. I got the call from university to say that I was not successful in my application as I did not have enough UCAS points. Once again, I was disheartened, thoughts of being dumb and thick came flooding back. However all was not lost, having spoken to the a member of staff from the University's outreach and recruitment team I was given two lifelines, the first to do a degree in Working with Children and Families with the possibility of doing a masters in social work or looking into an Access Course then re-applying for university. I looked into both avenues and weighed up the pros and cons against my young family, responsibilities and finances I opted for the Access Course. Although I lacked confidence and had self-doubt in bucket loads which my tutor called "the black dog" my tutor guided me and reassured me as did my husband that I could do this and succeed. After many late nights and deadlines, I got my grades and successfully passed my Access Course and got offers from all of my university choices. This was only possible due to the moral support from my husband who shouldered more of the household responsibilities to give me the extra time that I needed, and the support from my college tutor who took the time to breakdown assignments and explain them to me.

Fast forward to enrolment day, we had the option to enrol online or in person. I chose to do this online as it was quicker and easier due to family commitments. During the enrolment process I was given the opportunity to complete an optional online assessment to identify any additional learning needs, thinking nothing of this assuming that if I did have additional needs it would have been picked up in school, I completed the assessment for the sake of it. I was then emailed to say that based on the assessment I may benefit from an appointment with the Educational Psychologist and that they would contact me in due course to arrange this. The appointment took a while to come through and I was almost three months into my course and had been given my first assignment. No matter how hard I tried to understand the assignment I struggled and found the level of support at university in comparison to college was very minimal. I struggled with this to the extent that I sat in the course lead's office and looked at dropping out of university because I was struggling with understanding the assignment. The tutor took their time to look at the assignment with me and explain the question and asked that I at least give it a try before claiming defeat. So, I did.

Finally, my appointment came through and we talked about my educational history, what support was made available and conducted a series of tests. When the results came back as being diagnosed with Dyslexia and Dyspraxia, I was a little shocked to say the least and remember asking the Educational Psychologist "so all this time I wasn't dumb?" to which she said "not at all, you just didn't have the correct support." The comment from the Educational Psychologist gave me a new lease of confidence and reduced my self-doubt just enough to believe in myself and continue with my studies after she explained the different types of support I was entitled to such as an academic tutor, extra time in exams, staggered deadlines, and extensions to name a few alongside the relevant equipment that may be useful too. With the support from my academic tutor, I was able to identify strategies to help me with my studies. The best strategy I found for my learning needs was to write a plan for each assignment that highlighted each learning objective I needed to meet, bullet points of what I would include in the sections and any resources that I could use as a reference from lectures, reading lists, research and self-study. All my lecturers were happy to look at a plan which I used to my advantage and would add as much detail as possible almost as though it was the skeleton which I could then add flesh to and like a to do list, I would highlight the parts I had written about to avoid duplication thus staying within my word count.

All was going well when it came to the academic side of my studies and even my first placement went well as they understood my needs and were able to support me. I faced some issues during my final year while on placement as I felt that my learning needs were not understood by my practice educator. My final placement was with children's social care in a duty and assessment team. On the duty and assessment team I was completing the child and family assessments for any referrals that came through and had a deadline in which to complete them by. As I got more cases to manage and the workload increased, I adapted what worked for my assignments to use on placement. I would have lists of things I needed to do or follow up for each young person or family I was working with, this worked for me as due to my needs I struggle with focusing on many things at any one time. My practice educator felt that due to me having these lists it was as though I viewed my placement as a "tick box exercise" and was not taking it seriously. This is a comment that was made at my mid-point review and was not mentioned prior to this. At the meeting I explained that this was something that I found helped with my Dyslexia and managing my caseload which had proven to be effective as I was praised for the way in which I was working, adhering to deadlines and managing my caseload given that I was a student social worker. My placement tutor from the university was very supportive during this meeting highlighting that my needs were mentioned in my placement application and support plan. I was fortunate to be surrounded by people who were supportive and gave me the boost in confidence that I was able to successfully complete and pass my placement and then go on to graduate as a social worker.

I will forever be grateful to the university for having this screening tool as part of the enrolment process as without that I may not be where I am now. My diagnosis was my lifejacket that helped keep me afloat even in the stormiest of seas and with a combination of the support it provided, some hard work and determination from myself I was able to reach my destination and continue on my journey.

On the periphery of neurodiversity?

- Anonymous

A personal reflection. I have written this as someone who values reflection, to explore some parts of my journey so far. I hope to emphasise the value of individual differences and neurodiversity. Maybe aspects of my personal insight might resonate with others. Our communities of both practice and lived experiences are important.

Last year I went off sick from work with my first episode of mental unwellness. I had emotional and physical burnout having lived in a self-preservation stress response for an extended period of time. I have reflected that one of the influencing factors to becoming unwell was the long-established coping strategies that I employed from a young age. I am highly organised, I am very dedicated, I rarely failed to meet deadlines, I aimed to deliver unrelentingly high standards of work, and I sought external validation. I have built a career on a sense that my professional worth is the result of what I do, how well I do it, and in part what others think about my work. With multiple contributory aspects and the context of the pandemic, the difference between what I was achieving and what I believed was needed of me resulted in a sense of failure and shame. Over time, my self-esteem became linked to quite a critical internal self-dialogue. My deep thinking and feeling brain was kept busy until my mind-body system demanded a break.

Whilst I was off work, I made time to focus on my needs and to reflect on how I experience different environments. I even learnt how to just sit. I now recognise my own sensitivities more overtly and I continue to educate myself to support sensory sensitive family members. Rather than having a neurodiverse diagnosis, I have identified as being 'quirky'. My mum used to affectionately call me 'Phoebe' in a nod to the character in Friends. At primary school a few experiences led to me having an ECG. The Doctor said that something was 'not right' in my brain, with an inference of mild epilepsy, but it did not warrant a treatment response. We don't know what we don't know, and I grew up as an 80's child thinking that my processing and routine interactions with the world were fairly standard. I say that now in recognition of my evolved social work understanding of the uniqueness of each lived experience.

As I grew up the more obvious differences in my lived experience became the headlines that shaped my childhood. I was also academically capable and regularly interacted with a number of different households. I learnt how to adapt to different physical environments with different peoples. As a social worker there are times when I have felt like a chameleon in my ability to do this within various contexts. I am naturally an introverted person who has learnt extrovert capabilities. In alignment with a trans-generational narrative of 'get our heads down and work hard' I became competent in behaviours that are societally associated with social and professional success. I had a loving, supportive, and accepting network. My awareness of my 'quirky' brain faded into the background as my awareness of characteristics such as class, social mobility, and achieving independence increased. I had some fun adventures and gradually settled into adulthood until I found a professional 'fit' with social work.

I had never had an extended period of time off sick before. Becoming unwell was an opportunity for me to work towards wellness and to reflect on how I process information. I can have reactions to bright lights, loud sounds, and strong odours. Sometimes I also have strong feelings of anxiety or being overwhelmed. There are of course layers of influencing factors that impact on our lived experiences and wellbeing. These can include our familial factors, grief and loss, stress and trauma, as well as our individual characteristics. From a feminist perspective, gender is significant in terms of how we experience 'load' in our daily lives. However, I now also see connections that I was previously unaware of in terms of my processing and the world around me. I have a greater understanding of simultaneous truths. I worked hard on my recovery and was glad to return to work relatively quickly. I started to recalibrate and adapt my approach, to weigh my commitments against my immediate capacity. My goal is to stay within the limits of my resources, to rarely (if ever) use my contingency reserves, within the acceptance that no resources are infinite.

Rather than previously embracing and understanding how my individual brain worked, I managed to make it 'fit' in a more mainstream way. Until it didn't. Being highly sensitive is not associated with a diagnostic label but it affects how people engage with their wider worlds. Whilst it is not unique, estimated to apply to up to 20% of people, it is different to the assumed majority. Crucially for social work, highly sensitive people are often able to create strong connections with others, to build relationships based on meaningful empathy, and to think deeply about what might be happening in someone's life. We really care. Practitioners who are aware of their vulnerabilities know that tricky moments pass, and they know how to dig deep when needed. I may be on the periphery of neurodiversity, but I am trying to afford myself the kindness that I have always tried to offer others, in relation to what I need both personally and professionally.

Growth is not linear, but I am committed to nudging forward. I am a social worker and I believe in the potential of growth through change for us all.

My close and trusted colleague helped me to think about how this reflection might be received and perceived. Might it be used to pigeon-hole my experience within a generally neurotypical context? Would my so called 'scars' then be more visible than my deeply embedded resilience and capabilities? Might I thus be thought of for my fragility rather than my strength? I choose to submit this anonymously in the hope than one day we can all share our stories without the fear of professional repercussion, negativity, and marginalisation. We are relatable in our humanity. I stand with all those whose lived experiences gives them particular individual insight within this profession that we genuinely call home.

Going under, rising above, staying afloat: Doing a PhD in the time of Covid

- *Yulin Cheng*

I know that doing a PhD is going to be a hard and bumpy ride but what I have not prepared for is the overwhelming feeling of debilitating defeat and emotional fatigue, the loneliness of being surrounded by people in the field who do not share your values and whose expertise lies in pathologizing and dehumanizing human differences, the anger that consumes every second of my life confronting the neoliberal academia system that reeks of privileges and ableism, and the exasperation of living in an increasingly authoritarian country that demands conformity. The combination of this makes it a very hostile and alienating environment for anyone doing a doctoral study on neurodivergent rights and well-being that critiques and challenges dominant positivistic and scientifically 'objective' methods of research. Considering then the emotional labour that is required and demanded of a doctoral student with lived experience, is it no wonder that I am stressed and burnout?

The worst of all is that my PhD started in the months just prior to and leading up to the pandemic. More than half of my four-year PhD program was spent under a period of strict border control and quarantine restrictions. Trapped in a small city with overseas travel out of the question, I had not seen my parents in Singapore for 2 years and 10 months, and I have not had a holiday vacation (by this, I mean a break away from my research work) for more than 3 years. Whilst I have been spared from Covid infection, my mental health has suffered tremendously.

Being autistic, I need wide empty and solitary spaces to decompress and recover from the relentless pressure of living in what we called the modern life. Unfortunately, I had not realized how important this sensory need is to my well-being until after getting diagnosed with autism in my late twenties. Prior to that, I had built my life around the city and tried to live up to the standards of the culture and society I grew up in. I accepted and internalized the norms of the survival of the fittest as the way life should be. At the same time, having travelled to countries such as Australia, I was lured to the country's vast open spaces and wide blue skies. Having a place that I could go to and wind down, spend time away from crowd and enjoy solitude was crucial but a luxury. Australia is my driving force, my solace and haven. But as world travel came to a halt during Covid, so did my world and time.

I am studying under the department of "Social Work and Social Administration." The name itself is telling of the emphasis it places on management and governance as it runs like a corporate organization whose foremost concern is achievements and productivity above values such as social justice and ethics. Even during this unprecedented period of social unrest followed by the pandemic, there was no mention of how our students were coping health- and study-wise. Universities are no longer safe spaces for engaging in political speech and expressing dissenting opinions. The institution is complicit in and contributes to the systemic oppression of marginalized population and the stigmatizing of social problems. It seemed to have not occurred to the department that we are doing research in unprecedented times that is likely to affect our progress and necessitate more flexibility. For example, prior to the onset of another wave of Covid outbreak, our department issued an email to students claiming there was nothing to worry about and forbid non-local students from returning home (unless for research purpose) on the grounds that they were receiving stipend from the government and therefore had to remain in the country. This was unnecessarily rigid and devoid of compassion given how volatile the situation was at the time. On the other hand, the person who made the statement saw nothing wrong to excuse himself from wearing a mask in lecture halls and enclosed spaces for no reasons other than he didn't like it, in display of his arbitrary use of power and the lack of regard for other people.

I began my PhD program in September 2019 in the midst of a series of political protests. I had just returned from my annual vacation to Australia the month before and a few months prior to the outbreak of the virus in China. This is my fourth and final year (supposedly). I am expected to graduate by the end of August 2023 but my progress has been excruciatingly slow. I am struggling with my cognitive functions and worn out by antagonism, I'm not sure if I can submit my thesis and graduate on time, or even complete my study at all.

None of this is helped by the fact that I have a supervisor who is a boss more than a mentor and who was indeed my boss in my previous role as a research assistant. When I asked for help with my data analysis, he would delegate it to other research assistants under him as though it was covered in their job description, which I doubted. When I talk about confronting the system, he is the person I have in mind (and others like him). Our relationship is marked by increasing tension and resistance as I am less than 6 months away from my expected graduation and I have not been able to produce any significant progress.

For someone doing social work and mental health research, he has made several disparaging and ignorant remarks about qualitative research, and disrespectful and insensitive remarks about certain groups of minority populations in my presence. In my opinion, his disregard for lived experiences makes him unfit to be working in this field.

In January 2020, we ushered in the Year of the Rat with a worldwide pandemic. A year later, I was due for my probation presentation scheduled for the end of January. I wanted more time and asked to present in February, which would still be within time schedule, but he went ahead to schedule for January, ignoring my preference. He also did not consult my views on the reviewer he invited to my presentation despite knowing my apprehension and negative sentiment towards the autism researchers in our department who took a diminishing view of autism. The reviewer for my presentation is someone who has described autistic people as lacking in empathy and emotions. I took up the challenge but after working tirelessly days and nights in the week prior to my presentation, I still did not feel up for it so I asked to postpone my presentation to three weeks later. Instead of recognizing that I was on the brink of a breakdown, he continued to dissuade me and insisted it was for my benefit to get it done earlier rather than later, disregarding how I was actually feeling at that time. I thought that if I were to call myself a self-advocate, this was the time to advocate for myself. I wasn't going to let the guilt of postponing and rearranging override my needs, and even though I succeeded in my request, the fight I had to put up to assert my rights destroyed what little trust I had left over this department.

When one has to resort to putting their mental health on the negotiation table as a bargaining chip for reasonable accommodation, what does it say about how the department treats their staff and the values they teach students? When a system prioritizes grades and performance over all else, one quickly learns that mental health is something that can be sacrificed.

During the presentation, in my eagerness to explain the various stereotypes, stigma and prejudice that the society at large held towards autistic people, I overran my presentation time, in which I was criticized by the reviewer for my poor time management. In addition, the audiences questioned my use of online surveys and the ability of autistic people to answer them, which felt like a slap in the face after all that explanation I did. I felt defeated and alone defending myself.

A sense of loneliness overcame me that day and it terrified me. As someone who enjoys solitude and being alone, it was not a feeling that appeared in my vocabulary prior to that day. I wrote this in my diary,

"I reach my hands out, only to find that not all injustices are shared, so I pack them into my bag and walk away."

That loneliness has stayed with me since.

Since the pandemic in 2020, I have felt like stuck in a time warp. I missed my parents and my haven. As travel restrictions around the world were easing in early 2022, Hong Kong maintained a strict Covid zero policy. The first sign that things were beginning to look up was when they removed thc mandatory hotel quarantine requirement in October 2022. Immediately, I booked my return flight to visit my parents whom I last saw in January 2020. Since then, things have been moving fast. I have just co-authored my first editorial, two of my collaboration projects were accepted for poster presentation in the upcoming INSAR conference in May, I have been invited to speak about neurodiversity at the ITAKOM conference in March and another conference in April, I will be contributing a chapter to a book on psychology and mental health as a person with lived experience, and my contribution to this collection, to whom I'm extremely indebted to the publisher for giving me this opportunity and allowing my submission post-deadline. Somehow, I got to deal with these on top of my PhD thesis, which is already behind schedule. I wish these opportunities would have come in the earlier stages of my study but given that there is nobody else in my department or institution doing the kind of research I'm doing, I have to forge my own social network and connections through social media. While I have been somewhat successful in this respect, I am still in a bad place - physically and cognitively. I feel bittered that Covid has stolen my time. I have been stuck in a motionless carriage for nearly 3 years and all of a sudden, I am riding in a bullet train. Things are now moving so rapidly with multiple looming, extended and overdue deadlines, I'm worried they are heading for a crash.

With multiple impending deadlines, there is hardly any time to take a break and it doesn't seem like a good time to go on a break. Nonetheless, I haven't had a break for more than 3 years, I haven't had any recourse to release the stress and negativity that has been building up, I wasn't in a right state of mind, in fact, I have been hardly functioning.

In the last month, I had set aside two days to work on my article for this collection, but it was unproductive and the only paragraph I was satisfied with was my opening,

"I so desperately want to have a voice, to challenge institutional systems, to trouble academia, and to expose hypocrisy; to tell you how the education system has left me traumatised, the process of finding and losing myself; my regrets and unfulfilled dreams so you have a better idea of who I'm and why I'm the way I'm. And it's frustratingly ironic that I haven't been able to put my thoughts into words."

My executive and cognitive functions are failing me, I couldn't think, I couldn't cope and I'm struggling to keep up with my responsibilities and obligations. I needed to go away, I needed a change of surrounding, and none of my overdue deadline was as overdue as a trip to my haven. And so, despite my busy schedule and time-sensitive obligations, I booked a short 5-day trip to Australia and stayed by a quiet coastal town in the state of New South Wales. It wasn't so much a holiday but a much-needed mental health break as it has been 3 years and 7 months since my last vacation in Australia. I had wanted to use this opportunity to think and plan things through, which added some pressure for it implied a hope, if not, expectation that I would come back from this trip with a clearer and refreshed mind, or even some deliverables in terms of solid results. At the same time, I wanted to just leave my work behind for a few days and to spend time walking around exploring new places.

I can't say I left Australia with a less confused mind nor did the trip resolve my problems. Nonetheless, the day after I returned from Australia, I suddenly had a flow of ideas pouring in and what you are reading now is the result of that stream of ideas. It maybe that the trip hasn't helped me to think and plan things through entirely, but I will remember the excitement of my first day of arrival in Australia, the anticipation of being back for the first time since Covid and the joy of returning to my haven. What this trip has done was to remind me of what it's like to feel alive and to actually want to be alive. I am carrying these touching and heartfelt moments with me, holding on to them for as long as I can, and what this short break has given me is the strength I needed to move forward.

Coming out as autistic can be a risky move in some professions, let alone calling yourself a student-activist or scholar-activist in countries with limited freedom of expression. I am possibly the first openly autistic academic in Hong Kong. I want to, because I need to forge connections with autistics in the international community. And I am able to, not because I am bold and confident, but because I'm already in my 40s and I remain financially insecure with no promising career ahead, facing an unknown future - I have nothing to lose, there's nothing to lose. I have a monotropic mind that is moving at a pace that is too slow for this rat race I'm forced to run in. I'm not sure how things will turn out in the coming months, but I know the months ahead are going to be an intense roller coaster ride on turbulent waters. I know not what victory looks like, but I will try as best as I can to stay afloat no matter how seemingly impossible. I want to narrate my own story and to make use of whatever academic privilege I still enjoy to contribute to part of the neurodiversity movement and give voice to a population that has been unfairly and unjustly treated for so long.

This is dedicated to my Walden, thank you for being my safe haven and inspiration for this essay.

Dyslexia doesn't define me: Journey to success built by resilience, focus and creativity

- Pete Nevison

Let's paint a picture of where I started, what the world looked like as a child and young person. I grew up in the 1980's and 1990's where neurodiverse needs were a problem to society and children didn't get the screening and support that they needed. I dare say that neurodiverse people still don't get the support to maximise their potential. However, there has been significant improvement in how society have come to view this over the last decade. I came from a Dysfunctional household where my parents didn't behave in a nurturing and supportive way. At school teachers wrote me (and my family) off because of my parent's behaviour and due to my struggle in school, labelling me as 'lazy', 'thick' or 'not academically able'. The school would take me out into a 'special learning' group. I was about 13 before I could tell the time on a clock.

I knew that I was different to other children and that I could not pick things up in the way the mainstream education was taught but I didn't know why or how to succeed. I was often made to feel stupid which caused me to attempt to mask my needs with the skills I had built. This allowed me to cope or hide my needs from people, at least to a point. I even copied other children's answers to avoid looking stupid in class. I was never provided a screening assessment for Dyslexia at school or provided with any additional support from them, my family, or my workplaces as I moved through into adulthood. I left school without any qualifications that would allow me the progression and appraisal, that I so desired, which would also help me to build a successful career. I felt like life was hopeless when I left school and as I left, the dysfunctional nature of my family collapsed my life. My alcoholic mother died just as I turned 18 which left my other siblings at the mercy of the system whilst my father remained an inappropriate adult. I felt broken and lost as an adult, well I was an adult at least on paper, the world felt bleak. At this point I found myself worrying about money, having a place to stay and what would happen to the only parts of stability I had.

About 6 months after the death of my mother I started a role as a filing clerk in the banking sector that I secured via a temping agency. I delivered files to qualified advisors for them to assess for any compensation for pension mis-selling. I spent a decade building my skills without a qualification to become a project manager in the bank I worked. I still lived with the shame of my Dyslexia which I didn't have a formal diagnosis of but suspected it was there. I feared returning to education and more so to fail. It was easier to hide my difficulties than face the reality that I needed help, guidance, focus and most of all to realise I had built strategies. This might not have been all about my neurodiversity but a mixture of that and how people had perceived and treated me over the years. Had I been able to realise my Dyslexia sooner and obtain support, I may well have succeeded faster and without prejudice. At the point of becoming a project manager, I still didn't have a usable qualification to my name and as I said, I was frightened to return to education to reframe my potential. Many of the jobs I'd applied for over that period resulted in psychometric testing and I couldn't pass these tests which slowed my progression, however, it didn't stifle my desire to better myself. The banking recession of 2008 caused my job to be put at risk, it was time to re-evaluate my options with the potential of redundancy looming.

I spent my life hiding my difficulties so that I could blend in, feeling embarrassed about my difficulties instead of embracing my strengths. I was 28 and this was my moment to step outside of my box, all be it brief. The embarrassment, lack of confidence, low self-esteem and my self-critical nature would hold me to ransom for several years yet. It is important to say though, this is the tipping point, the time I made the move to better understand myself. I took a skills test that helped me think about what I might be able to re-train as and Social Work was one of the top scoring areas for my passion and skills. I then paid for an educational psychologist to assess me and finally obtained a diagnosis of Dyslexia. This was the first major leap I took to understanding myself and to challenge the world around me. I had skills but I needed the formal qualifications to better my future and show people my innovative thinking was worth more than they realised.

It is important to accredit some of this story to Leeds and Bradford Dyslexia Association (LaBDA, now Yorkshire Rose) because they directed me to the psychologist and talked things through with me. After my diagnosis and report I knew what areas I needed to develop. I started to undertake some voluntary work with them in order to teach Dyslexic children how to touch type using specialist software. I quickly realised that I could use this software to teach myself how to touch type, I was a one finger man up to this point on a keyboard. I used this Dyslexia friendly package, I feel this is called English Type, to teach myself how to touch type. This is the single most effective skill I have taught myself and it has become invaluable with regards to my ability to work at speed and improve my spelling. I still cannot spell well if I write things down though. I returned to undertake my GSCE English and a level 2 in maths, followed by an Access Course. By sharing my assessment and recommendations I was able to obtain reasonable adjustments, something that I had never been able to access before because I'd never had any diagnosis. However, now for the first time I knew my developmental needs and difficulties as well as my strengths. I still wasn't confident to openly talk about my Dyslexia but I was making progress.

These reasonable adjustments along with building on my strengths and focusing on strategies for my difficulties, allowed me to engage with education and the workplace in a different way. I finished my social work degree with a 1st class honours and promptly started my journey as an ASYE in the local authority where I have since done 10 years' practice. Now, I'd like to say that I embraced my neurodiversity and showcased my skills during this time. In part this is correct, I have indeed showcased my strengths and creative thinking, for example, being able to turn complex data into simple spreadsheets and visual diagrams. I have been able to reframe approaches, point out commissioning gaps and recommend ways to improve services. My thinking allows me to consider the wider picture and evaluate how we can improve the journey and experience when people need help. However, I have failed to promote these strengths as being part of my neurodiverse thinking until very recently. Why? This is a good question at this point. The simple answer is I still feel shame about being Dyslexic, shame because I am different, because I need strategies and at times reasonable adjustments. Shame because I want to read lots of books, but I just can't focus for long periods or read quick enough to digest the materials. Maybe this is a mixture of shame and embarrassment. This part is why I hide my Dyslexia, why I'd tell people who needed to know that I am Dyslexic but then counter this with, "I have good strategies." I guess the point I should champion is that I shouldn't feel this way and in fact workplaces need to change. I'd go one step beyond this, if there is a profession that should be winning at promoting this, it should be Social Work.

More recently I have been applying for senior roles and I've quickly learnt that just because organisations say they have 'disability confident' employment status, doesn't mean that they apply that criteria or think about the tools people need. I didn't think about this, I state I am Dyslexic on an application form but never give much thought as to how the potential interview will apply a 'reasonable adjustment.' During the last decade and before I have spent my life telling people, "I have good coping strategies so you can't even see my Dyslexia." This is my default statement because I don't want people to use my Dyslexia against me like it has been in the past. It has recently caused me not to be clear in interviews around reasonable adjustments and what I think would be reasonable for me, considering my processing speeds and working memory. This doesn't absolve organisations from any unconscious discrimination. I have learnt from these experiences.

I have undertaken neurodiversity training, asked to become part of the staff disability network and started to champion a new way. This here is my next major turning point, you see up to now I haven't challenged or promoted the importance thinking differently for those with neurodiversity, or presented with pride about the unique attributes I hold. I decided that I needed to make sure that people knew what neurodiverse people can do. Importantly, I proactively started banging the drum for people to think about strengths and reasonable adjustments and how organisations apply the disability confident criteria. This isn't the time for hiding and society certainly needs more understanding and Social Workers must fly the flag for neurodiverse people. At this point in my story it is 2022, I am 42, so it has taken my 42 years to realise that this isn't my issue and in fact it is my strength. The tide needs to turn. Interviewers and employers can be inclusive and champion their disability confident schemes by taking some time to think and check in with the person. They can provide materials ahead of meetings, training, or interviews. If there's a timed element to allow for the working memory and processing speeds, in real life there are natural pauses, or you can take questions away. However, these points are specific to me and every person with Dyslexia or another neurodiverse need is different.

In summary, my experiences do pose many questions and here are a few. What about all those people who don't have a formal diagnosis? What about all those people who also were impacted by historic bias and have not had any screening in school, or the workplace? What about all the people who still slip through the net that become affected in school and during their careers? Maybe employers need to screen their staff to provide at least a diagnosis and some idea of useful aids and approaches. What value do you get from timing interviews? Is that the best way to assess skills for job vacancies? A final parting note for thought, I have recently moved organisations, into senior role in a new organisation. I am making waves in my career, I am moving forward and I celebrate my successes. Organisations and employees need to do more in order to fly the flag of neurodiversity, not just tick a box. Think about the strengths, creativity and resilience people bring to the table. You can frame to opportunities of getting some great skills from neurodiverse people in your teams, organisations. You can grow and retain those individuals too. So, if you are reading this and you are Dyslexic, neurodiverse or you suspect you are, fly that flag and seek your potential. If you're an employer think about those questions, the workplace isn't a test it's an opportunity to grow the best talent to meet your objectives.

A hidden disability: Being a social worker with an acquired brain injury

- Caroline Aldridge

I have no memory of how I tripped on the stairs and banged my head, or of my hours in 'resus' afterwards. I have just a vague recollection of a ride in a spaceship followed by days that merged into each other after I was discharged. I do remember vividly my confusion and frustration in the weeks that followed. I also remember working hard at trying to find strategies to overcome my difficulties with cognition, memory, speech, sensory processing, and balance. And, if I am honest, I developed ways to hide how much my brain was malfunctioning. My husband recalls that, even in A and E, I did not want people to know my brain might be injured. When asked very difficult (in that moment) questions, such as 'what is your date of birth?', I replied evasively - 'I do know the answer to this, I am a social worker and I have a very good brain.' I had clearly absorbed the idea that acquired brain injuries (ABI) are A Very Bad Thing. In the five years since my accident, I have learnt that having a brain that works differently has its limitations but also created possibilities. In this chapter, I will reflect on my experiences of a largely hidden neuro-disability and consider potential benefits to the social work profession of being more inclusive.

My fears about brain injuries came from somewhere. All our attitudes and assumptions about everything we encounter as social workers do. I had no particular personal or professional experiences to draw on so I probably formed my ideas from colleagues, reading, films, and the media. There is very little information for social workers about ABIs which is one reason why BASW (2019) created some guidelines. I found the information from Headway to be the most balanced and helpful (www.headway.org).

If you do an internet search for 'social worker' and 'brain injury' the results will be about social workers working with service-users who have an acquired brain injury not social workers who have one. I would like to think that with social work priding itself on non-judgemental and anti-oppressive practice, any work-related articles I stumbled across would be balanced. However, an assumption that people with ABIs have changed personalities, are violent, have difficulties with relationships, and are disinhibited, abound. The outcomes for people with ABI are reportedly poor. In a Community Care article, people with ABIs were described as often 'selfish' and 'egocentric' (Eggington, 2013). It is easy to see how having an ABI and being a social worker might be incompatible. I suspect that when we read about ABIs it is a more extreme (and stigmatised) end of the spectrum that features.

No surprise then, that when friends and family tried to tell me that they thought my concussion was a more serious issue because they observed some of my difficulties, 'brain injury' was not a label I wished to acquire. I can remember being horrified when my GP suggested referring me to the neuro-rehabilitation team because I was still presenting with symptoms.

In the acute phase of an injury, which can last several weeks, the brain is still bruised. For me this presented as extreme fatigue, difficulties in concentrating, speech aphasia (inability to find words), issues with my balance (vestibular system), and visual perceptions. Simple things like planning and preparing a meal were hit and miss. I only needed a distraction and I would forget what I was doing. I could hold a 1:1 conversation about quite complex work or academic related things but I was unable to retrieve and use common words. I quickly found work arounds, such as using synonyms, to prevent embarrassment. Although I developed strategies at home, for example checking with my hands where walls or doorways were so I did not walk into them, I was unable to function out of the house. I would experience sensory overload and be unable to balance, or think, and I would feel nauseous. What I did not realise was my strategies were counter-productive. I needed to retrain my brain to do things, by avoiding them or using alternatives I was exacerbating my problems. An example of this being the strategy I used of holding someone's arm to maintain my balance. This meant my brain was not learning for itself how to remain upright. Although I lacked insight into the extent of the damage to my brain, I had enough to know not to attempt to drive or go out without assistance.

Once the bruising had receded and I realised I had ongoing problems, things in many ways got harder. I started worrying about whether I would ever be recovered enough to work because I was still struggling with physical and cognitive issues. By the time the neuro-rehabilitation consultation came around I was so grateful to finally be assessed. I had realised I was not going to recover without help. I entered to world of 'service-user' which was not easy. I was referred to speech therapy and given exercises to do such as trying to hold a conversation with 3 or more people or to play word association games. A friend suggested I join a small creative writing group to help with these things. Even though I could not concentrate on writing for more than half an hour, I found myself writing a memoir. The referral to the vestibular clinic to work on my balance probably made the biggest difference because it gave me my independence back. The first time I was able to go to the supermarket unassisted I felt such a sense of achievement.

I was referred to an occupational therapy group for people with brain injuries who wanted to return to work. That was helpful but also sobering. I think the purpose of the group was really to get us to accept we would not be returning to our careers. Sitting alongside the NHS manager whose speech was incoherent, the engineer who couldn't use his hands, and the businessman who needed to live with his parents because he couldn't meet his own basic care needs, I felt fortunate. I realised there were still many things I could do. When I shared that I was writing a book in the hope of building skills and returning to my job as a social work lecturer, I was met with some gentle, but pointed, comments about the way brain injuries can reduce our self-awareness of our limitations and the need to be realistic. On reflection, I think they thought I must have some frontal lobe damage that was giving me false perceptions of my abilities. In fact, I did regain my computer skills, write the book (Aldridge, 2020), and return to work.

One of the most useful things I learnt from the occupational therapy group was about pacing and Spoon Theory (Miserandino, 2003). I think we could all benefit from applying these ideas and using our energy wisely. I had been lurching from 'boom to bust' in my activity and fatigue levels. Mistakenly thinking I was building up stamina, I would try not to nap and keep going but this would be followed with days where I could barely function. Accepting that taking naps meant I was able to be more productive felt counter-intuitive but it really helped manage my fatigue levels. Spoons theory suggests that we have an optimal number of 'spoons' of energy in a given day. Following a brain injury these are reduced so we need to choose how to use our energy to best effect and rest so we can replenish. I was using lots of energy doing basic tasks like washing, dressing, or making the bed. By switching my day to working in bed, having a nap, then getting up, I was able to achieve more.

10 months after my accident, I returned to work part-time. I still had considerable difficulties arising from the brain injury although mostly these were not noticeable to others. I had been assessed as fit to drive but due to fatigue could not drive far, walking was exhausting, stairs a hazard, and unfamiliar or busy environments could cause sensory overload. However, occupational health were brilliant and they recommended 'reasonable adjustments 'under the Equality Act (2010). My managers went the 'extra mile' and let me focus on where my strengths lay. Looking back, their faith in me was remarkable and it also was pivotal in regaining my confidence. I wrote a successful bid and then designed a social work apprenticeship programme. It was many more months before I could manage the busy environment of a classroom. At every step of the way, my teaching colleagues supported me to do what I could, helped me when I couldn't, and accepted that my ability to function was variable. I wish I could say all my social work colleagues were as inclusive. Some were kind and supportive but I had numerous embarrassing and humiliating conversations where stating that I had a disability, which required some adjustments, led to either intrusive questioning or ignoring my requests.

Like many neuro-diverse people, my functioning can be context specific and my disability is largely hidden. Most of the time I function as if there is nothing wrong. When I am tired I can get a return of symptoms. I can present as a bit odd or appear 'drunk' when sensory overload occurs. This can make me anxious in unfamiliar settings and I still rely on someone trusted to help me navigate. If I need to speak at a conference or deliver training beyond my near and familiar environments, I need someone to get me there, orientate me, and support me. In some situations, I would be a liability without a carer. For example, I am unsteady and under-confident on stairs and if there's lots of people and/or noise in a stairwell my ability to know where to place my feet plummets. Risk assessments of people with ABIs generally centre around people's insight. I guess I was lucky that, once I adjusted to having a brain injury, I have insight into what poses a risk to me or others. Without this I would have been one of the stigmatised group of people with ABIs who are viewed as a series of deficits.

Some things that were damaged when I hit my head are gone forever. There are gaps in my memory; numbers and dates mean very little to me; I make more typos; and I cannot multi-task. I have many strategies to help with these things. Each morning I set a series of alarms to remind me what is coming up. I have lists (and lists of lists), I double check things and ask for help checking things. I use the camera on my phone to help me. For example, photographing landmarks to remind me where I parked the car or things I need to remember. The ability to teach or hold meetings virtually has helped enormously in overcoming my issues with travel or busy environments. However, the visual and auditory distortions make it tiring. I prefer to have something static on the screen to focus on like a PowerPoint because there is less for my brain to cope with. I wish people would not use fake backgrounds because they are visually distracting. Because I find multi-tasking very difficult, I cannot keep up with fast 'chat', looking at multiple screens, or looking at emails and messages whilst in virtual meetings.

Some of these things might be viewed as negative. But it is all a question of perspective. I do not multi-task and I have to focus carefully, therefore people have my full attention. I am single-minded about my areas of interest and do not waste energy doing irrelevant things. I genuinely think that having to find alternative pathways in my brain has opened up areas that were dormant or under-developed. I seem to be able to intuitively connect things that previously I might not have noticed. My brain has developed in some areas of strength and my ability to critically analyse, go into a topic in depth, and my strategies for retrieving information have been finely honed in the last 5 years. Because I need to structure and plan things in detail, I think things through and pace myself which has improved my ability to organise projects and deliver to deadlines.

I think my creativity has been enhanced because I have to find different ways of doing things to accommodate my quirky brain. For example, I can only manage a limited number of hours of computer time so I developed ways of using textile arts for reflection and expression. My empathy and insight into living with neurodiversity or a disability has exponentially grown.

I would not have chosen to have a brain injury. Sometimes I get upset about the things I cannot do anymore or I feel exhausted. But having a literal 'bang on the head' has changed the direction of my life. Had my husband not been home to call an ambulance I would probably have died from blood loss. I feel profoundly grateful to be alive. Having to re-evaluate what was important to me has meant I prioritise how I spend my time and energy.

I do wonder what the consequences of an ABI been had I still been working in front-line social work. I am not convinced these pressurised working environments could have accommodated the adaptations I needed. I would have had skills, knowledge, and professional wisdom but been hampered by an inability to drive far or safely manage going into homes and other environments. There must be other social workers, or potential social workers, with brain injuries. It seems to me it is a loss to the profession if we do not find ways of including them. For a whole host of reasons, they could bring benefits but they might challenge the system to be committed to making adjustments that enable and include. In my opinion, if employers made adjustments that would benefit their neuro-diverse staff all their workforce might benefit. Imagine working in an environment that is sensory calming, with the possibility of focussing properly on one task at a time, and taking proper breaks.

Maybe we need to ask ourselves how we react and support people with brains that are neuro-diverse and how inclusive social work is. A good starting point would be to question our own knowledge of, and assumptions about, ABIs. We need to embrace the strengths and possibilities that neurodiversity can bring to social work.

References

Aldridge, C. (2020) *He Died Waiting: Learning the Lessons – A Bereaved Mother's View of Mental Health Services.* Norwich. Learning Social Worker Publications.

BASW (2019) Understanding People Affected by Brain Injury: Practice Guidance for Social Workers and Social Care Teams https://www.basw.co.uk/system/files/resources/181036%20Understanding%20people%20affected%20by%20Acquired%20Brain%20Injury.pdf Accessed 12.3.2023

Eggington, S. (2013) *Why Social Work is So Important for Brain Injury Survivors.* https://www.communitycare.co.uk/2013/01/29/why-social-work-is-so-important-for-brain-injury-survivors/ Accessed 12.3.2023

Miserandino, C. (2003) *The Spoon Theory* https://cdn.totalcomputersusa.com/butyoudontlooksick.com/uploads/2010/02/BYDLS-TheSpoonTheory.pdf Accessed 12.3.2023

Welcome to my World

- Kathryn Chorley

So... My mother has ADHD traits, and my father is Autistic, but both have been unaware of this until recently. They kindly passed these 'Neuro gifts' to me, and their grandchildren.

Sadly, for me, being a super hyperactive, impulsive, and inattentive child in the 1970's caused major shame for us all.

But thankfully, Neurodiversity awareness has changed over time the grandchildren understand; and are comfortable with their differences and manage them well. They have the view that its ok to be a bit weird and have a lovely freedom to talk openly between themselves about their traits.

For me, school was hell, but adulthood and work was ok once I realised that I could do jobs that complemented my ADHD and Autism traits. For example, working night duties by myself in a children's home. I could organise things in a certain order all night long, without much interference, which suited me well. I used the quiet times to read and learn more and more facts, which is something I love. I also worked with people who had nursing needs and older people who had Dementia. I applied to be a nurse a few times when I was younger but couldn't pass the entrance maths exam – I suspect that I have Dyscalculia.

When I was 32 years old, my daughter Jess came along, and I quicky became a single parent without any means of support, emotionally, practically, or financially.

Panic set in, and I made the very solid and rigid decision to bring her up myself, get a university degree, provide for her myself and never live with another man until the parenting job was done.

Random thought – I have always been convinced that my ADHD presentation is much stronger than the Autism, however that is not how this story is sounding is it ??? (laughing).

Anyway, I think I made some good (but rigid) decisions along the way for me and Jess; and she turned out great and happy. I found going to university was hard, especially with my ADHD related difficulties – but I had an excellent tutor called Gavin who really helped me a lot with extra tuition and guidance here and there.

After my Social Work degree, I was thrown into Child Protection for years, which was highly stressful and often confrontational. Caseloads were high, and sadly there was very limited time allowed for each child. However, looking back, I am proud of the work I did and the respect and compassion that I offered no matter how volatile or upsetting the situation was.

Over time, the cost to me emotionally was immense, I had good relationships with the children I worked with, and I worried about them. The unpredictable nature of the job meant that after taking annual leave, I always dreaded logging back on or checking my mail, because I knew there was a real risk that something could have gone very wrong for any of the children allocated to me.

As an Autistic person, I can be overly empathic, and managing unpredictable changes is not my greatest strength. This impact was so apparent that when I left Children's Social

Care, to work in a much more predictable and stable post – I found that I still dreaded logging back on after Annual Leave and opening mail for years afterwards, even though I knew nothing worrying would be there.

When I left Children's Social Care, my manager said that she never felt that she had to check up on me because I was so rigidly organised, and although I had grown to dislike the job, I was good at it, so I should stay in my post, or risk losing my skills.

No chance I thought, I've done my bit... but even though I felt half dead and used and abused by the hard-core social work system and culture; I received a lovely complement that that alleviated my rejection sensitivity.

I'm easily pleased, aren't I?

I then moved to into child and adolescent mental health (CAMHS) and did 2 years University post grad training in Systemic Family Therapy.

I found that this wasn't for me – my rigid brain needs a much more solution focussed format, rather than all the formatting stuff used in therapy. Thankfully, I ended up on the front door of CAMHS and found that the Neurodevelopmental initial assessments suited me very well. Perhaps because I could identify with the 'lively' children and parents. This work prompted training in Neurodiversity, and this led my subsequent specialism within the Neurodevelopmental Team.

By this time (age 47), Menopausal night sweats had collided with my ADHD insomnia, causing a period of massive hardship and exhaustion. I thought that HRT would help, but I was allergic to it, and it caused a Pulmonary embolism that nearly killed me and took me a few years to recover from;

even though I went back to work after a few months. So, for those few years, I had a lung injury, night sweats, permanent exhaustion, and a Neurodiverse teenager who was terrified that I might drop dead.

Fast forward a few years, I was aged 50 and still (Neuro) undiagnosed, just living with it and masking the traits; enduring most days and only looking forward to bedtime.

Due to the work that I was doing within the Neurodevelopmental Team, I had suspected that I had ADHD for a few years. But this really became 'real' when my then 17-year-old daughter Jess was diagnosed with ADHD and Autism. The decision to pursue a diagnosis was driven by Jess's feelings of isolation in her own Neuro- diagnosis and her sense of fairness.

I remember her saying, "you need to get tested, because you are way worse than me."

Bit rude I thought – but a fair comment, so this popped me into the good old precontemplation stage.

Then, I was then blessed to be assigned a student social worker who has ADHD herself, when I became a Practice Educator. I think I learned as much from her as she learned from me, and she focussed and encouraged me to sort my own Neuro assessment referral out.

I love a certificate...and I got 2! One for ADHD and one for Autism.

I now have a Neurodivergent friends' group, who have backed up and validated my thoughts about my own traits. It's wonderful to have similar friends who have similar traits and similar interests, and our lack of masking when together is a breath of fresh air.

So... here I am, physically healed from the past, I'm doing a job I have a personal and professional passion for, and this blend is so helpful in understanding the perspectives of the children and families that I work with.

Life is now good, so is ADHD medication.

Massive thank you to my lovely Jess, and my best friend Darren who took over as her dad when she was 18 months old and helped me bring her up.

Also, thank you to my wonderful friends and family who have supported me, thank God for you all.

A short reflection as a Social Worker living with ADHD & OCD

- Hannah

From my own research, I have discovered that the term "neurodiversity" was first coined in the late 1990's by a sociologist named Judy Singer (Chapman, 2020). It is interesting that this phrase has existed for 20+ years, yet from my experiences, many professionals in Social Work practice seem to not know what the term neurodiversity means or have limited understanding around this. I qualified as a Social Worker July 2021, and since this time more and more Social Workers seem to feel able to come forward and share their narratives as professionals living with conditions that fit under the neurodiversity umbrella. I am pleased that this movement is happening, and that this book is being created to give people like myself the opportunity to express what life is like for us as neurodiverse Social Workers, but to also help those who may feel they are different from their neurotypical peers, or that they don't fit in the profession, to feel confident and know what great Social Workers they are.

I have suffered with OCD since I was around ten years old, and ADHD as long as I can remember. The way I interacted with the world, and my ability to socially interact has always been different. I even remember in high school being given 1:1 "Social Skills" lessons to help me with friendships. As a child, many of the adults in my life described me as difficult to emotionally connect with, and my mother found it challenging to deal with me and certain behaviours I exhibited such as not listening or being extremely sensitive. I had a difficult childhood, going into foster care at the age of ten. I feel that for those who are neurodiverse, adverse experiences can cause amplified trauma. But I also feel that adverse experiences are more commonly experienced by us, due to the way we interpret and interact with the world. We can be more sensitive to rejection, and often face ongoing criticism. As someone who was on the child protection register for emotional abuse, was that just due to my mum's mental health problems, or was that also because I was more likely to be subject to criticism as a child with ADHD?

I will try not to digress but will say that my ADHD particularly made academic pursuits harder, for example obtaining my Social Work degree. This was due to difficulty with time management and organisation. My dissertation was extremely overwhelming, and I felt I lacked the skills to complete a project so huge. Of course, I did do this, but it felt like it took all the brain power I had to do so, and I took a lot longer to complete this than most of my peers. In my role as a Social Worker, such difficulties continue. I completed my ASYE in child protection, a frontline team which felt extremely chaotic, and by the end of this I was completely burnt out. It got to a point where my brain just felt like it was going to explode, and I had headaches most days. I did not know how to organise, or plan to complete all the visits I needed to do and meet all my deadlines, and every time a new crisis came up it threw me. I'd repeatedly turn up to supervision with my manager asking me "have you done this?" and I'd realise I had forgotten yet another task I was meant to have completed. I made endless lists to try and help me to keep on top of my workload, but nothing seemed to help.

For us who are neurodiverse, it takes a lot more effort to do every day work tasks, which can also depend on if our brains decide to function on a given day. Personally, my energy levels, social battery and overall brain ability fluctuates, so one week I may be able to keep up with my workload, but the next I may get myself behind. I don't want to dwell on my time working in child protection, but I will say there was little understanding around neurodiversity, and how reasonable adjustments can make such a positive difference. I was made to feel that being neurodiverse, having difficulties with organisation, writing, keeping on top of my workload etc, meant there was something wrong with me, and that I wasn't cut out to do the job. I didn't listen when colleagues told me that the chaos, never-ending paperwork, high case load is the same everywhere in Social Work, implying I wouldn't manage working in another team if I was struggling in frontline... I left anyway and got a job in fostering.

Since no longer being in a team which is crisis led, I have been able to not only enjoy my role more, but I've been able to accept myself as someone who lives with ADHD and OCD. I have adjustments in place and am able to manage my own diary to ensure I can do my job well and avoid burnout. For example, I make sure I spend time working from home to recharge my batteries, or if I'm not feeling great. I'm not forced to go into the office every day, where there is often loud noise and distraction which means I then can't concentrate on my work. More importantly, I'm not made to feel that my differences are a burden and mean I'm less competent as a Social Worker.

I am open about having ADHD and OCD within the workplace because I do not feel either are anything to be ashamed of. In fact, I previously have supported children with ADHD, and it felt more special because I knew I could understand them a lot better than Social Workers without ADHD perhaps could. I have had colleagues who have openly voiced how ADHD is simply a reaction to trauma, almost invalidating the condition. I do feel that more needs to be done in Social Work to truly understand conditions such as autism, ADHD, Dyspraxia, Dyslexia, OCD etc. Social Work strives to be an inclusive profession and needs more diversity and people whose brains work in all kinds of wonderful ways. Many of the people we support are neurodiverse, which makes it even more important for Social Workers to have an understanding around this. I think it is amazing that neurodiverse groups are forming across the country for Social Workers in the profession, and this is something I have put forward to the equality, diversity and inclusion lead within my local authority.

To conclude, neurodiverse colleagues should not suffer in silence or doubt their abilities just because how they interact, or practice may not be considered conventional or the "norm" by those who are neurotypical. Social Work is a profession which should welcome everyone and recognise the talents that those with neurodiversity can bring such as creativity and "out of the box" thinking, amongst many other things. I personally think difference is always great and gives opportunity for learning. If we were all the same life would be boring! With that in mind I am looking forward to learning more about others who are neurodiverse and can't wait to read the narratives of everyone who has contributed to this anthology.

References

Chapman, R. (2020) Defining neurodiversity for research and practice. *In Neurodiversity Studies* (pp. 218-220). Routledge.

Searching for missing puzzle pieces: in a squiggly world with a touch of colour

- *Karen Gilbank*

I used to wonder whether I was a puppet, whether this was all just a game. Were we all individually designed for a purpose? Like the song by Aha – "Take on Me" where the cartoon comes alive, coincidently there is a motorbike in that song too (you will get what I mean later).

As I struggled to find my way out of the maze, I always felt I was stuck in (and I have never been any good at real life mazes I cannot work out direction at all – is London up North?), it wasn't until 43 years later that I had some real answers and understanding of who I am.

I was not disappointed to be diagnosed with Autism and ADHD, in fact it was a huge relief.

Finally, I was beginning to find the missing puzzle pieces in my life.

I am going to write about my experience as a neurodivergent social worker. I will try my best not to digress too much but no promises as this tends to be one of the things, I excel in.

Once upon a time (this is how all stories start, right?) my mother was in labour with me, the only transport my dad had available was a motorbike, so that's how we travelled on the back of a motorbike, true adrenaline fuelled style and I was born crying and screaming.

I should make you aware that this is no fairy tale story.... or maybe it was, there is always a good and evil character in fairy tales and the ending is usually positive, so yes then maybe it is a fairy tale (promise broken, sorry).

For 43 years, I have found life a struggle, always feeling like I was different to other people, that my brain would be always running like a treadmill with no stop button. Sometimes I would press the emergency stop button as I would be exhausted and need to hide away from the world. My thoughts were deep, I questioned everything even the random stuff like why I am me and not somebody else? and wondering what the purpose of life was. Fast forward to now and at the age of 43 I was diagnosed with ADHD and Autism – I finally felt like I belonged and could be my true self, quirks, and all.

As I was growing up, I never felt like I truly connected to anything or anyone, I was aware that I would try hard to fit in with others although this was exhausting. I spent a lot of time daydreaming in my bedroom looking out of the window observing people and their behaviour, fantasising about the fact that they could be criminals or up to no good. I loved drawing and my mother often reminds me that I wouldn't start drawing until I had lined up all my pens in colour order. I also did this with sweets that were different colours. I had certain rules that I had to follow, that I had made up, no one else ever knew, they were my thing which I guess reflecting upon now helped me to stay in control of my life to some degree.

In social situations I was filled with anxiety. I would try and make myself less noticeable and was always the person you would see standing in the corner. I hated being put on the spot and if I was, I would repeatedly replay scenarios later that had taken place and how I might have been perceived.

I put in place what I now know to be safety behaviours for example always needing to have my bag on my shoulder or a pen in my hand (I still use the pen in my hand now).

My favourite times were when I spent time alone in our local fields pondering life and what it meant. I would sit in the long grass hiding and feeling like I had escaped the busy overwhelming world. I think I have always been a reflector and spent a lot of times in the fields thinking about life generally. I loved watching the clouds and trying to see what shapes I could make.

I became a master at masking, no one ever asked if I was OK, I think I just felt unnoticed. I would be called dolly daydreamer as I had no urgency for anything I didn't enjoy. However, I seemed to have a great ability to hyperfocus on the things I was interested in for example anything that meant I was organising or putting things in order.

I also loved playing football or running – I had lots of energy for these sports, and I guess in some ways there was no requirement for social conversations as there were rules to follow. I love rules and boxes which is something I have carried through to my working life. I seem to love telling people that I like written things in boxes, must be something to do with how I process things.

I hated speaking to anyone, particularly.....well anyone really. As a teenager I questioned everything but could never find out the answers. I sometimes felt like I was two different people, at home I would be confident, and in school I was very shy and quiet. I did OK at school, but I put everything off until the last minute. I understood everything literally (I still do now). I never felt like I fitted in. If I am honest, I hated school, mostly upper school as it was so big and terrifying with lots of people. There was a time when I just didn't go to school, it was easy then as schools never contacted parents. I once took a whole week off hiding in my friend's wardrobe (it was a walk-in wardrobe) we would get a duvet and just chill out. Previously we would just sit in her bedroom however the window cleaner gave us such a fright when his head popped up that we decided the wardrobe was safer.

I applied for college after my GCSEs however this did not last long. As soon as we were told we had to do a presentation, my brain said no. I left and began working in a factory where I would always be blamed for things that went wrong – I never had the confidence to stand up for myself which actually reminds me of primary school where a teacher accused me of chewing gum, with the fear that I felt (and I still remember the teacher's name) I was unable to speak so ended up having to stay in at break time. If only I could have spoken up and said that I was chewing my actual gum (cheek). Anyway, I digressed again.

Eventually I was made redundant at the factory and took a post in a law firm, funnily enough opening post. I still didn't know what I wanted to do career wise. I stayed in this employment for 13 years....why? because I was just too scared to go for an interview anywhere else. I worked hard and eventually began to work up the ranks and was promoted as a legal trainer. You are probably thinking how the hell did you do that when you were so scared of presenting to people. Well, I had learnt new strategies, for example, not looking at people when I was talking, trying to make things as practical as possible so that I wouldn't need to stand at the front and using humour where I could – I felt like I needed to make people laugh. I think I still carry that now, but you can be the judge of that.

I knew I didn't want to do this forever and decided to embark on a social work degree. This brought up new challenges, part of the interview process was to have a joint discussion with other applicants whilst being observed. I rehearsed what I wanted to say, and I didn't care when I said it or whether it fit in with what someone else was saying I just said it knowing that to pass this part you just had to be involved. I made it on to the course!! I had to re-do my maths GCSE and I also had to complete a foundation year. This was another challenge – we went away on a residential and had to do a group presentation. I literally broke down in tears, I just couldn't do it, I let my anxiety consume me.

My tutor spoke to me and said that sometimes we have to set ourselves challenges and put ourselves outside our comfort zone and that it will get easier with time (I can honestly say 14 years have passed and presentations have never got any easier for me... until I was diagnosed and for some reason this has increased my confidence). I had to do another presentation during the social work degree (again I rehearsed one thing I would say, and I just said that line irrelevant of whether it was the appropriate time). Reflecting now, I really wish someone had shown more curiosity about what might be going on for me, but there is the problem, people's views of Autism and ADHD can be very stereotyped and go unnoticed especially for females. Therefore, I am open about my own diagnoses as I want to challenge perspectives.

I have now been in Social Work for the last 10 years, firstly working in the Local Authority and currently for the NHS as an Advanced Practitioner Social Work Lead. I have always felt that I have had to work hard (x100) to prove myself as a competent practitioner. I struggle being told good things about myself as this puts additional pressure on me to keep up to that standard.

I am aware of all my little quirks my stimming which is something I do unconsciously but then become conscious about it as I am doing it. Some of my stims include rocking backwards and forwards, pulling my fingers through my hair repeatedly and messing about with my hands or fidget ring. This helps me to regulate my emotions in the busy world. I also struggle sensory wise with bright lighting. My colleagues know me well enough and are very accepting when I ask to switch off the lights. Certain sounds are very overwhelming for example people chewing food, coughing repeatedly, people breathing (only joking), people having meetings online without headphones. I usually put in my ear plugs to drown the noise out.

I can struggle to leave things unfinished, and it will play on my mind. I do like having structure and routine, but this is mainly with work. My handbag would tell a different story which would include words like chaotic, messy and dare I say disgusting especially since I most likely have the entire contents of a cutlery drawer which has not been washed in a while sitting in the bottom of my bag.

In my personal life it can be chaos to some degree, I never finish anything, I start a project but get bored quickly and am distracted. Over time I am trying to be more accepting that I can't achieve everything, I feel validated since receiving my diagnoses which I think in turn has had an impact on my confidence. It is funny (except it is not) that I only seriously questioned the possibility of being neurodivergent when my children were diagnosed. For years I was described as someone who would get overwhelmed easily, however that's not how I saw it, I just needed to know things in more detail so that I could complete the job to a good standard.

I think as a neurodivergent Social Worker I do have a lot to offer – I might not sit with my colleagues to have lunch (I often need a recharge alone in my car) but I always try to be supportive, caring and empathic. In some ways I feel very lucky, that somehow, I had built up resilience and strategies to manage to get to where I am – I could never imagine at the age of 13 thinking that I would be in the role I am now supporting students and staff, presenting to universities and services.

There are some things that I promote with people that I work with and that is professional curiosity, kindness, and empathy. These are free tools for everyone to use. I have found these skills to be something I have personally developed naturally. I do however have to be self-aware that sometimes kindness and empathy can also be a weakness for me as well as a strength. I must keep an eye on my battery levels and ensure that I recharge by doing something nice for myself for example going to a spa (and not speaking to anyone).

At the age of 44 I now feel more confident and comfortable in myself, I have friends that are neurodivergent and we just get each other. I haven't necessarily sung from the roof tops about my diagnoses, but I am not ashamed of who I am. All I would advise people is that if you know that person that may come across at anti-social or interrupt your conversations or want to do something a certain way, be curious about why that might be. Always ask why and then repeat again and again. I always try to accept people the way they are, after all it would be a black and white world with only a couple of types of personalities. I much prefer the touch of colour in a world that is a bit squiggly.

So, all that was left of the social worker who was nearly born on a motorbike in transit, was to find that last missing piece of her puzzle, she begins the search by reaching for her handbag.

The end.

The Importance of Chasing a Diagnosis and Accepting Yourself

- David Grimm

Trigger Warning: suicide

For 22 years, between the ages of 12 and 34, I have lived with suicidal thoughts. Almost the entirety of that time, each day I'd wake up actively making plans. Some days I was so crippled by the fight that I couldn't move, act or engage in life.

Since I was 15 years old, all I have wanted is to be a father with a happy household, and/or to commit to the grim reaper. Those were my two goals in life, with smaller goals in between as a distraction, but those were my top tier. Doctors have thrown antidepressants at me since I was a hormonal child, but none of it stuck. In fact, most medication made my ideation heavier and increased my conviction to try, so when I did try and didn't succeed, my depression and guilt of failure just engraved deeper into my soul. All of that with no success.

Recently I paid for a private assessment of ADHD, with a hail Mary attempt at an answer to why I was so deeply broken and guess what?...I have ADHD *shock horror*. Most days since, I've been lost and unsure of who I am, BUT NOT SUICIDAL!

24 years of makeshift, guesswork medical and psychological approaches...deepening my already existing issues through misdiagnosis. Making me feel crazy when all it was, was a different way my brain chemistry is wired.

I know this won't be the same for all...but considering the government are endlessly speaking about mental health and suicide prevention, I must say that this diagnosis has been tremendous in helping me and must be worth investment and research.

I've had an incredible life with incredible and loving friends and family, I've seen lots of the world and I'm at university. My life is full. Yet I was still suicidal, and it may potentially come back but I just want to say that it's nothing to be ashamed of please just ask for help.

My ADHD diagnosis hasn't fixed all of me, but I wake up most days content...I pray that more and more children receive help and appropriate diagnoses before they are adults and suicidal.

I feel lost without that feeling, how messed up is that. but I'm so much more at peace because someone believed me and helped me see the answer.

An imposter in the neurodivergent world?

- Chris Norman

If anyone had told me that I'd be sitting here writing a piece to go into a book about neurodiversity, I'd have been very sceptical, yet, here I am. I have to be upfront at this point, I don't have any kind of neurodiverse diagnoses and in my life, it's never been mentioned as a concern during formal education, which bearing in mind I'm no spring chicken, would suggest that my input into this book shouldn't be necessary. Recently however, I've found myself becoming aware of neurodiverse conditions and being told by those with experience, that I 'fit' the profile. This, coupled with a conversation with my eldest child who has had similar thoughts about their own experiences has led me to question more and dig a little deeper.

My whole life, I've always felt that I'm a bit different to 'normal' people. I mainly put this down to being an only child and not interacting with kids in the same way as others did. I just felt that life hadn't given me the opportunities to learn the same skills as most children did and as such, this made me unusual. I was always said to be an academic child with expectations that I would do well in my learning and get good results but I was always boringly average at best. I found this frustrating as I constantly felt that I wasn't achieving my full potential. My school reports invariably said that I should "stop staring out the window" or "work a bit harder." I was never very good at focusing in class, always distracted by something else but not usually overly disruptive, perhaps because as an only child I wasn't used to having other children to be silly with. I found that I would either be vague and lost or completely focused and would get the work done in a very short time but without the attention to detail that I knew I was capable of. At school, nobody ever raised any kind of concern that I was falling behind but I never achieved what I felt I should be capable of, and I still feel this way in my current studies. I always assumed that I had delusions about my abilities and should adjust my expectations which is what I did throughout my life, accepting the mediocre as my best.

As an adult, I met someone who has become and remains hugely important to me, and has instilled a level of confidence and self-belief that I didn't know was possible. That individual's faith in me and encouragement has led to me studying social work, passing my degree at a good standard and moving on, to study various things at Masters level, both work related and independently with another distance learning degree to complement my current knowledge.

On my journey into social work, I've met many people who are neurodivergent with conditions such as OCD, ADHD and ASD. Learning about their experiences and the ways in which they have strategies to manage their learning and other needs has made me evaluate my own learning as many of those experiences and strategies mirror my own. I had just assumed that these were things that everyone did, the list upon list of the tasks that need attention both at work and home, being unable to focus on something until my brain has had enough subconscious processing time, being all or nothing in my writing of essays or assessments being a few examples.

To be honest, this has both surprised and scared me as it had never occurred to anyone in my life that there was something actually 'wrong' or different about me. The more I've thought about it the more I've become both certain and confused about my experiences. I'm still not sure I should be writing this as I feel like a total imposter here but I'm told that it might be helpful to others which is a good enough reason to carry on.

I find that I swing between not being able to get motivated and functioning on a task to being so hyper focused that I get it done in super quick time. I've learnt to use the times of day when I tend to function best as windows of opportunity to achieve the things on my many lists. I've taught myself to (mostly) not talk over people although sometimes this still happens. I try really hard not to go off on weird tangents because my brain has gone somewhere entirely different to the topic at hand. I think adulthood and some level of maturity has helped me be more aware and analytical about how I am with others and why I should do/not do certain things to fit with social norms.

Friends who know my recent conundrum about investigating my possible neurodiversity further, know that I'm struggling to analyse if pursuing a diagnosis would help me or not. I can see that I do appear to have a lot of the traits associated with ADHD and this is what my eldest child independently thought that they have so the familial link could be there. I can also see the traits in one of my parents too which would suggest the genetics are there.

I always associate neurodivergence with artistic and creative traits and this is not a way that I would describe myself generally, although I played several musical instruments as a child (sadly time prohibits this now), so perhaps I am?! I find my creativity through cooking, which I love to do, although I wouldn't include this as an artistic type trait. I often find physical activities and sports hard to coordinate which is a frustration as I process these things very slowly which my brain hates but my body can't keep up and it doesn't seem to do what I want it to, for example, I constantly mix up my left and right which means that I do things with the wrong hand (not great in some sports).

I tend to see my skills and abilities as a cross between a blessing and a curse. The curse being when I get stuck in a cycle of poor motivation and the blessing being when I'm able to get through huge amounts of work in a short space of time. Sometimes I think it would be nice to be more balanced and able to work at a reasonable pace all the time rather than the boom or bust style I seem to have. Despite still being undecided about whether pursuing a formal diagnosis will help, I would say, if symptoms are having a negative impact on your life and ability to achieve what you believe yourself to be capable of, talk to someone. Whether you just find strategies to help yourself or you seek diagnosis and perhaps treatment, do something about it so you don't continue to be stuck and not fulfilling your potential.

I think that social work is a profession where a lot of people experience imposter syndrome, I know I have, initially as a student, then again as a newly qualified worker and now, I'm experiencing it again as I've taken my first senior social work role. The thing I love about social work is that it brings such a variety of individuals to work with, situations to analyse and experiences to gain, that it suits my personality (and perhaps my 'ADHD'?) because there is never a dull moment, there is always something new and challenging to do and the pace suits my need to be constantly doing different things to avoid boredom. Personally, I think that social work is an amazing career choice, especially if, like me, you are a people person, and from what I can see, it fits well with neurodiversity for many individuals. So, perhaps I should dispel that feeling of being an imposter in this conversation?

Zebra

- Sandy Symonds

I read a tweet on Twitter a while ago by the 80's singer and songwriter Alison Moyet, sadly her account has been deleted, it read something like this: *in a field of horses, it is good to know that I am a Zebra*. This really chimed with me. I love the visualisation it brings to mind. It sums up the notion that those of us who are Neurodiverse are in many ways similar but are also seen differently within the norms of society, and I can certainly identify with this as an idea and in my experience.

I grew on a nice working-class estate in the south-east of England. I started school in the very late 70s and left school in the mid-80s. Most of my memories of infant school and junior school are positive. I didn't have any sense of feeling different, they were nice small schools. Each year I changed class teacher as all children did as we moved through the school. From approximately the age of nine I changed class, but not with the rest of my classmates. I was moved into a different class some distance away from all the other classes. This class was much smaller with a range of different aged children. I didn't know the children in this new class. As I recall we had different break times to the main school. As I think back now as an adult this was my first experience of feeling different. There was no explanation given for the change, I remember thinking I must have done something wrong to have been placed away from my friends. This class was referred to as the 'remedial class', thankfully not a term used now. This was a class for children with special educational needs. Not something to be ashamed of, however, because of the way the change had taken place, how we were segregated and perceived by the other children, I felt ashamed. All I knew was that I struggled to read, and subsequently struggled with spelling also. This was explained as me being 'lazy' and 'distracted'. Change was coming within education to prevent this practice but, sadly not in my time-frame. The Warnock report in 1978 adopted the term special educational needs and recommended the end of remedial classes, those with special educational needs would remain in their classes with their needs be met by the class teacher (Warnock, 1979).

By the time I moved on to secondary school things were quite different. The secondary school was a large comprehensive school with a wide variety of other schools feeding into it. Due to its size and the much larger classes, it was easier for me to hidc in plain sight and not be singled out as different too often, which by this time was all I wanted. I remember just wanting to be average, not to stand out in any way for anything. My school reports carried on highlighting that if I was to just try in class and be less lazy and distracted things would surely improve. I felt different. I was trying very hard to catch up, and it was so confusing to try to understand why I struggled with these tasks, that my peers seemed to manage with such ease. One particular example was in English classes where the teacher would go around to each pupil expecting them to read a couple of paragraphs out loud to the whole class. As I attempted to read, badly, tripping over the spellings the other children found it hilarious. I found it humiliating. Bit by bit my confidence and sense of self was eroding away, I became more and more introverted. I struggled to make new friends in school and became rather isolated. Quite the change from the confident happy young child at the start of junior school to a rather miserable and unhappy young person by the end of secondary school. I struggled through to the end of secondary school, I came away with my GCSEs, not the best grades but the best I could manage in the circumstances. Any prospect of going on into further education didn't seem to be an option and by this time I just wanted to go out into the world of work and not have to navigate an educational environment again. My school education experience had quite a significant impact on my confidence. I know that my experience is not that unusual. It is important to remember that this was the 1980s and things have changed considerably in education now.

Within the world of work I gradually rebuilt my sense of self as I grew into a more confident adult. At the age of 29 I was at a bit of crossroads. I'd had some interesting employment opportunities but nothing I really considered as fulfilling and not exactly a career as I saw it. I was pregnant and this became a great time of reflection for me. Thinking about what my child might become and the experiences he might have, I found myself reflecting on my own childhood and my own experiences for the first time really. I remembered having a careers advice meeting at secondary school. The careers adviser fed all my interests into a rather cumbersome and now very dated computer program, and it concluded that I should consider a career in social work. I had a couple of friends who were already undertaking the social work course and it did spark my interest and fitted with some of my more recent work experience. I applied to three different universities, attending the interviews in varying progressions of my pregnancy and to my surprise was offered a place at each university. I had my son in the March and started university in the October of the same year. I felt it was important to start the course that particular year because it was the final year that the social work course remained as two diplomas. The diploma in higher education and the diploma in social work. The following year it was due to change to the degree course. I couldn't imagine that there would be any prospect of me completing a degree, and the course at the time I felt was more practical than that of an academic degree (Grant & Hewson 2022). So that was my motivation to join the course when I did. At no point during the course did I really believe that I was going to pass. I focused on each essay and each placement in turn and didn't think ahead. At this point my Dyslexia had still not been diagnosed, I continued to struggle to read the vast amount of required reading and retain the information I had read. The university I attended was just at the cusp of switching over from handwritten essays to typed essays. I was incredibly lucky to have someone who could decipher my handwriting and typed up all my essays for me, that made a huge difference. I'm glad to say that I completed the course and my social work career started. Despite the struggles without doubt it was the right decision. The diploma in higher education element really helped me to catch up on some of the lost learning from school and my confidence slowly grew in my abilities.

As a newly qualified social worker I struggled with my own organisation, and at times became overwhelmed not only in relation to the volume of work but how to prioritise it. I struggled through knowing that it was an issue. It was an uncomfortable time, I worked hard to think about how I could get better at organisation myself and I tried lots of different tactics. When I think back to that time now it feels like a completely different practitioner. Organisation doesn't look like an issue for me outwardly now, although I still have to work it. Some years later I had the opportunity to undertake the practice education course. It was at this point my Dyslexia, Dyspraxia and my Irlens Syndrome (visual stress) were formally diagnosed.

Having my neurodiversity confirmed as an adult has been a bitter-sweet experience. It was a relief to finally understand why I had struggled so much in education, but not just that, also with other things in adult life too. It was liberating to read around my diagnosis, to recognise my struggles in the traits and to finally understand my difference, my zebra-ness. It is of course also tinged with sadness thinking about the time that had been lost in my education foundation, and the what if's. What if it had been diagnosed sooner? What if I had some helpful support what kind of career might I have? It has taken me a while to accept my diagnosis. I was introduced to the world of assistive technology. I was reticent to use the technology and in fact didn't use it very often at all. I felt embarrassed feeling it highlighted my difficulties. I have come to terms with it more and use the assistive technology more regularly. I continued my studies at university completing a master's degree. In the world of social work there are many social workers who have gained master's degrees, but when I think back to that very unhappy, confused and hopeless young person unable to see much of a future, I am very proud of my achievement.

Does having a label matter?

You don't have to be in social work for very long to experience the constant change and shift in the language and terms that we use. It is important that our practice is constantly evolving and responding to the increases in our knowledge and understanding. Focusing on neurodiversity can feel a bit like the next new thing, the next trend that we are all talking about. The more we are open, interested, and curious about individuals needs the better able we are to support both the people we work with and the families we support. For me it is all about the focus on acceptance and inclusivity. It doesn't matter if someone has a formal diagnosis of a particular condition or not. If they can recognise themselves as having neurodiverse traits, then it is about supporting that person to meet the goals that they are aiming for. We need to remember that the process of diagnosis itself is challenging and can carry an emotional cost. The process focuses so much on what an individual cannot do rather than what their strengths are. This is not necessarily something that everyone will be willing to participate in. We also need to consider the financial cost of diagnosis. There are often long waiting lists, and if looking to fund a private diagnosis the financial costs can exclude many people. Gaining a diagnosis should be a personal choice. It can be helpful in discovering particular traits and once having that knowledge being able to go on to find strategies and/or technology that helps to maximise skills and abilities. Having a formal diagnosis can also feel supportive, the opportunity to connect with other neurodiverse individuals, perhaps leading to a sense of belonging. The downside to focusing so much on individual diagnoses and "pigeon holing" a group of people as neurodiverse, can be to take away from their individual uniqueness. As humans we are all different with many similar and different traits, we need to be mindful of categorising different groups in society and the impact and unintended consequences this can have.

Having an inclusive culture matters

I feel it is important to address the stigma that can exist in the workplace preventing practitioners talking about their needs (Koutsounia 2022). From my own experience, and from working with social workers and social care practitioners, I know it can feel daunting, worrying and even embarrassing disclosing and discussing Neurodiversity traits with a manager, particularly if extra support is needed. Often the supervisor or manager can also feel uncomfortable not knowing what to say, worried that they will cause offence by saying the wrong thing. I have had my own experiences of these awkward conversations. I had one manager who I hugely respect who said on several occasions when complimenting my work that they felt, I managed well given my "difficulties". Initially I found this offensive but, quickly accepted that this was about a lack of knowledge and understanding. Even though I had discussed what having Dyslexia meant to me. I could see they felt awkward each time they said it.

I have seen a lack of understanding of what Neurodiversity can actually mean for other practitioners, and this can be overshadowed by a supervisor's own embarrassment of imagining that they should know and understand all about Neurodiversity leaving an uneasy situation where neither the practitioner's needs, or the supervisor's are being met. The supervisor does not know how to support the practitioner and the practitioner does not feel heard or able to say what support they might find helpful. Inevitably the practitioner tries to muddle through as best they can at somewhat of a disadvantage, becoming overwhelmed and stuck.

This in some way can be addressed by upskilling practitioners and team managers in understanding the spectrum of Neurodiverse traits, rather than just drilling down to any specific conditions as this will not achieve equality. Reviewing policies and procedures to ensure that they are Neurodiverse inclusive. Openly catering for those with Neurodiverse traits in training, meetings, and interview processes. This will also benefit all employees but, more importantly it will be bringing Neurodiverse traits into the open, encouraging conversations, connections and increasing acceptance and inclusivity, positively impacting on the working environment and culture for all. "...achieving inclusion and diversity means actions need to be part of an ecosystem approach, not a one-off campaign" (Smith & Kirby, 2021 pp223).

There is an opportunity here to focus on individual strengths, celebrating success and being less preoccupied with sitting in the deficit model. In practice we make time considering how to work best with families including what the latest research tells us and the best framework to use, and rightly so. Do we consider to a similar level how to best support practitioners undertaking the social work role? With greater emphasis currently on neurodiversity this is a chance to make sustainable change so that we value all our practitioners as the important resource that they are and appreciate and are grateful for all the diverse skills that we bring to our roles. The specific skills that those with Dyslexia traits bring can be seen as particularly desirable within social work typically including big picture thinking, the ability to see patterns in complex situations, creative problem solving and, 'explorative cognitive search', (Taylor & Vestergaard, 2022). It is important that the social work profession truly represents the communities that we serve. It is equally important that we value all social workers whatever colour or flavour their Zebra stripes might be.

And finally

I have to say embarking on the university course with a very small baby at home it isn't something I would necessarily recommend. As for the baby, well... my brilliant Son is now a thriving young adult. Who too has Neurodiverse traits and who has taught me a lot about living well with Neurodiversity and, I couldn't be prouder of him.

References

Gant, V. & Hewson, M. (2022) *Social work students and dyslexia: outcomes from an empirical study and some implications for practice*, Social Work Education, DOI: 10.1080/02615479.2022.2120192 (Accessed: November 27, 2022).

Koutsouna, K. (2022) *Neurodivergent Social Workers 'exhausted' by lack of understanding at work* Community Care. Available at: https://www.communitycare.co.uk/2022/08/17/neurodivergent-social-workers-exhausted-workplace-lack-of-understanding/ (Accessed: November 27, 2022).

Smith, T. and Kirby, A. (2021) *Neurodiversity at work drive innovation, performance and productivity with a neurodiverse workforce.* London, United Kingdom: Kogan Page pp223.

Taylor, H. and Vestergaard, M.D. (2022) *Developmental dyslexia: Disorder or specialization in exploration?* Frontiers in Psychology, 13. Available at: https://doi.org/10.3389/fpsyg.2022.889245.

Warnock, M. (1979) *Children with special needs:* The Warnock Report. *BMJ*, 1(6164), pp. 667–668. Available at: https://doi.org/10.1136/bmj.1.6164.667.

On becoming neurodivergent and holding onto my 'Ikagai'

- *Siobhan Maclean*

Twenty odd years into my career I was really happy with my work. I was working part time in practice and part time as an independent trainer and practice education consultant. The Japanese concept of Ikagai was new to me but made a great deal of sense. The Japanese believe that Ikagai is about the intersection of what you love, what you're good at, what the world needs and what you can be paid for. The belief is that leading a life where these four domains connect gives a person a sense of purpose and a reason for living. I felt that I had found my Ikagai and life was good. Little did I know that life was about to change and holding tight to my Ikagai was going to be important.

Bang! And everything changes

I'd spent most of the weekend moderating portfolios when I felt like someone had come along behind me and whacked me hard in the back of my neck. The pain made me shout out (although I was on my own). Assuming that I had pulled a muscle in my neck, I took a couple of pain killers and went to bed – sleeping for something like 15hours. I woke up the next morning with a banging headache and a painful neck which got progressively worse during the next few days. Eventually, the pain got so bad (now I understand the phrase "a real pain in the neck!") that I went to the local minor injuries clinic. I don't really remember much else until I woke up a week or so later on a stroke ward. I now know that I had experienced a vertebral arterial dissection (the artery in my neck had spontaneously split) which most people do not survive. The bleeding artery had caused a stroke and I woke up unable to verbally communicate, I couldn't swallow, and I was confused about why my body wouldn't move.

The following few weeks are a bit of a blur and I am reliant on what my family and friends tell me about the experience. There are experiences from my time on the ward though that stand out in my mind. Listening to staff asking, "who is on the feeders today?" whilst standing at the end of my bed had a profound impact on me. The dehumanised, infantilised language used by ward staff stripped me of every sense of self; increased my feelings of vulnerability and sense of dependency. Over the next couple of months, I was assessed by two different social workers – once for a move onto a specialist rehab ward and once as part of the hospital discharge process. Neither was a good experience. The first social worker barely looked at me, all I saw was the top of her head and the back of a clipboard. I could tell that she was simply ticking boxes. She occasionally asked a question but didn't allow me the time to respond. I felt stripped of every element of my identity. I kept telling her that I was registered with HCPC (the regulator at the time) I suppose trying to reclaim my professional self. I tried to be clear that I wanted to be able to return to work, although my verbal communication was mixed up at that point and family tell me that I often described wanting to get back to being a teapot! so it may not have made full sense. I certainly did not feel listened to and was disappointed in my profession. I started to question my Ikagai – surely social work is about hope and here I was stripped of hope by social workers. The experience really made me question my sense of self.

I do know that I very clearly expressed my desire to relearn to read. At the time this was one of the most important things *to* me. However, this was in no way in tune with what the various professionals thought was important *for* me. They wanted to ensure that I could "independently mobilise up three steps" (their words not mine). This made no sense to me. I could return to work if I couldn't "independently mobilise" but I couldn't go back to work if I was unable to read and write. No-one seemed interested in helping me with that. If someone wanted to relearn basic literacy skills, who would you refer to? Maybe it doesn't link in with measurable outcomes and the tight criteria that everyone is working to nowadays – but that was the absolutely the most important thing to me at that point. The key to me relearning to read was actually a complete fluke. I have thought a number of times about what would have happened had the nurse that particular day put on her apron the right way around. Would I have ever realised how I might be able to read? In fact, the nurse put the red plastic pinny on inside out and I was able to read it. I was so excited that I was shouting out "Do not disturb drug round in progress" and laughing. I was excited to realise that I could read effectively 'inside out' but think that my response was interpreted very differently by staff.

Months later, I paid to access my notes, I was described (a number of times) as a "non-compliant patient" (I'm fairly sure that my recovery was greatly assisted by non-compliance.) I was also described as having 'tantrums'. One phrase written by a social worker was particularly disappointing - "*Needs to come to terms with what has happened. Support should be provided for this. Family giving false hope. She needs to understand she will not return to work. May not be able to do work of any kind.*"

I have always thought that hope is one of the most essential aspects of social work – the concept of hope was a key part of my Ikagai. According to Clark (2012) there are two types of hope: personal hope which is embedded in a wider social context and professional hope. A range of issues can impact on personal hopefulness - such as family, culture and personal experiences. Personal hopefulness can be strengthened by effective social networks and diminished by neglect, abuse and trauma. Professional hope is embedded in the professional value base and a belief in the possibility of change. My experience of being a 'service user' was that social workers were trying to distinguish hope rather than holding hope with me. I have recently found that when I am overwhelmed, listening to a poem (which I have on my desktop in readiness) is helpful. The poem called 'If This Time' by Kevin McCormack contains the lines "*If this time has taught me anything it is that hope matters and we cannot live without it. This time has taught me that hope is not a wish, nor a desire for something to be different. It is a course of action, a combination of mind and heart.*" I think I have always used hope as a catalyst for change and the driver for action. Hope has served me well and has connected with my Ikagai.

Understanding my 'new self'

As I progressed with my recovery the physical signs of a stroke were less and less. I could move around fairly easily, I couldn't wear heeled shoes as my balance was completely thrown by them, but honestly it would have been pretty difficult for anyone to recognise what my body had been through. The symptoms which I now recognise as neurodivergence were much more significant and I really struggled with these and learning about my 'new self' on a range of levels.

I remember the first time that we went out to a coffee shop. My head almost exploded as my brain tried to listen into every conversation in the room, the noise was deafening, and it physically hurt. I was waiting for my daughter to come back from the counter to tell her that I needed to leave when a young woman with a learning disability came in, she was smiling and communicating very excitedly creating quite a few sounds. I sat frozen to the spot. I needed to leave, but I didn't want the woman and the people she was with to think that it was because of her. Others in the environment were tutting and staring at the party and, acutely aware of the discrimination that people face, I did not want to add to this by leaving almost as soon as she came in.

My new struggles

The way that I now read means that I have lost the ability to read phonetically or to sound out new words. As a consequence, I really struggle with words that are new to me or that contain new sounds. I do a great deal of work in Wales and always feel really disrespectful when I fail to pronounce people's names correctly. There is one amazing social worker who I have known for years and I still can't say her name. As someone who is particularly aware of racism and committed to anti-racist practice I know how important it is to get someone's name right and I remain acutely aware of the potential impact of my struggle with this. It's not always easy or appropriate to tell people why I struggle to pronounce their name correctly.

I had been back at work for a few years and had adapted to my new skillset when I started to find things really difficult again. I found myself crying in the toilets of so many training venues, not really sure why, I was again losing words and experiencing a foggy brain, my emotions were all over the place and I was feeling very low. I was starting to experience the perimenopause. I found the medical response to this really inadequate. As someone who has had a stroke, I am not able to take HRT which really seemed the only medical advice. The Doctor simply told me that maybe work was too much for me after all. There were times where I questioned whether life was actually worth living. I think that holding onto my Ikagai and sharing my menopause experiences with friends is all that kept me holding on by a very thin thread! I have often reflected that I am glad that I was able to get through this stage of my life alive – it sounds dramatic but is very true. I am a passionate believer in menopause awareness, and I think the impact of neurodiversity in relation to the impact of the menopause needs deeper consideration.

When Covid19 hit and our ways of working changed one of the struggles that I had was amplified and I really needed support to tackle this head on. I have always found technology difficult and learning about new systems has taken me some time. When the pandemic first started and everything moved online I felt out of my depth and wondered whether I would be able to navigate this whole new world. I reached out on twitter asking if any students would like to help me to deliver some webinars to support students to keep connected with their studies during the lockdown. An amazing group of students (including Kelly my co-editor for this book) came forward and with their help I was able to develop the skills to deliver sessions online and manage the new technological world. The team (with a few changes along the way) are still acting as a support to one another and just last week I asked them for help with a computer issue I had. Their support has helped me in more ways than I think they understand. As the world of online delivery has developed almost everyone is developing their own system. As an independent trainer I am now asked to use and navigate so many different tech systems and I have found this overwhelming at times (I lost count at using more than 22 systems). I have recently developed the ability to say to people that I will use a range of systems but that I will not learn a whole new system just to deliver a presentation for them. I was worried about doing this but have found that when I explain the limitations that my stroke has created people are very understanding. When I first returned to work, I never mentioned my limitations perhaps because of fear and even shame. More recently I have been much more open, and I hope that encourages other people to be open with me about their own learning needs.

My changed strengths

Whilst having a stroke is not something that I see as a positive experience I hope that I have been able to take a strengths-based approach to the situation, such that I can recognise my strengths (some of which are new and as a result of my neurodiversity) and build on these.

Of course, everyone's strengths constantly change, but it is important to recognise that people who have had strokes will experience significant change which will be further impacted by the changes the human growth and development bring (the menopause for example has impacted on my strengths as well as my struggles).

I am able to fully focus on the work that I am doing. When I am with a person or with a group then I am fully focused on them. I am not trying to multi-task in ways that I used to, and I think this means that I am more able to connect with people, even with the challenges of virtual working. I have always thought that active presence in social work is important and now feel that I am totally able to bring that active presence. It does mean that I often have work that needs completing at other times making my working day longer and particularly as someone who is self-employed, I have struggled to get a work / life balance, but I think I am just about getting there.

Perhaps linked to the ability to fully focus, I have also developed skills in tuning into work more effectively. Whilst there are many references to reflection in and reflection on action in social work (Schon 1983) there are less references to reflection for action (Killian and Todnem 1991). Reflecting before action is important, tuning into what we are going to do is vital. With the changes to the way that my brain works, I don't feel able to 'wing it' now and I recognise my need to feel fully prepared for something. Previously, I might have seen spending time tuning into an activity as slowing me down, now I recognise that it is actually speeding me up.

I hope that as I have experienced significant change in my own self, I have become more aware of diversity and intersectionality. This is something that we try to be constantly aware of in social work, but the experiences that I have had and the way that (particularly medical staff) speak about me rather than to me has made me more acutely aware of the experiences of the people that social work supports. I wonder whether previously I took a largely non-oppressive rather than anti-oppressive stance in my practice. Prospera Tedam's excellent 4D2P model illustrates the difference between the two is 'disruption' (Tedam 2021) and I now wonder how disruptive I was. There are so many oppressive experiences that we have started to normalise in social work and I think I had become comfortable and perhaps complacent. Now I see the importance of disrupting the oppression that people face. Is that because of a resurgence in the importance of ideas around anti-oppressive practice within the profession or because of my experiences? Perhaps it is a combination of the two.

Certainly, my personal experiences have reinforced for me the vital importance of kindness. The Maya Angelou quote that *"people will forget what you said, people will forget what you did, but people will never forget how you made them feel"* is definitely true. Following the way that I was made to feel by professionals involved in my stroke recovery (both positive and negative experiences) I have started to understand the vital importance of kindness in professional practice. I am currently enjoying giving presentations about the importance of holding on to kindness in social work and working with Caroline Aldridge to develop ideas about kindness in practice.

My career has involved writing about social work theory for many years. When I was trying to return to this post stroke, I struggled to write very many words in a day and each day I found that I could write less as I needed to remind myself of what I had written the previous day. I had the idea to develop some short notes about theories in the form of 'flash' cards. These social work theory cards have become a popular resource and so I am able to see that a number of positive things have come out of my new strengths.

My hopes and fears

I started my social work journey 37 years ago. Lots has changed in that time and writing this reflection has helped me to think about my hopes and fears, both in terms of myself and the profession that I love. I genuinely believe now that social work is not just what I do but it is who I am so perhaps the hopes and fears are the same. I don't believe that there has ever been a golden era of social work. There have always been things that we have needed to do, but recent changes to social work education, training and regulation in England really worry me. The move currently is towards new standards to be called KSBs which detail knowledge, skills and behaviours. I have always referred to the knowledge skills and values that social workers need (whatever the standards of the day have been called – and there have been a fair few changes to this in my time). Now I am left asking myself what happened to values? I am concerned that social work is seen as purely statutory and that it is being diluted into a set of 'behaviours' and interventions. I hope that the profession stays strong and maintains a tight hold of the values which set us apart from other professional groups.

Perhaps my most central fear is that I have become removed from people. The pandemic has led to very significant changes to the way that I work. I spend lots of time alone now, talking to people virtually. When I press the big red button to end an online training session or webinar I am alone at home. In some ways this is really helpful to me. One of the things that I have needed to think carefully about since my stroke is 'interruptions'. I used to be able to sit in a busy office typing up case notes and reports, chatting away with colleagues. Now I have to concentrate solely on the task in hand. If someone interrupts me when I am writing, for example, it can take me ages to get back to where I was. Being alone is therefore helpful as I can ensure that my phone is on silent and there are no interruptions enabling me to focus on one thing at a time. However, the downside of this is that I am feeling very alone at the moment, a sense which has been amplified by changes in my personal relationship and a significant geographical move. I need to think about how to create more 'real life' connections. Being alone can feel psychologically safe in the short term but I know it isn't good for me in the longer term. I connect strongly with the idea of Ubuntu and know that people cannot exist in isolation. We become people through our connections with other people. I am glad that the decolonisation of the social work curriculum means that Ubuntu is more widely recognised as a vital "*philosophy of social development that can strengthen social work theory and practice*" (Truell and Mayaka 2021). In the new world of online working and so many social workers working from home, it is important to recognise that we are only people through other people, and we should embrace Ubuntu in contemporary social work.

Maintaining my Ikagai

Social work has always been my Ikagai – I love the role and the profession, I think I am fairly good at what I do, the world certainly needs social work and I am paid for my work. I have faced many challenges along the way but my love for social work and the fact that the world needs it has remained central – acting as my core. My advice to everyone involved in social work is to hold on tight to your Ikagai. Keep focused on why you came into social work. That will take you a long way!

References

Clark, E. (2012) Social workers are holders of hope. NASW News 57, 3.

Killian, J. and Todnem, G. (1991) Reflective judgment concepts of justification and their relationship to age and education. Journal of Applied Developmental Psychology 2(2) pp. 89-116.

Schon, D. (1983) The Reflective Practitioner. How Professionals Think in Action. (London) Temple Smith.

Tedam, P. (2021) Anti-Oppressive Social Work Practice. (London) Sage Learning Matters.

Truell, R. and Mayaka, B. (2021) *Ubuntu and its potential impact on the international social work profession*. International Social Work 1-14. DOI: 10.1177/00208728211022787 journals.sagepub.com/home/isw

POEMS

Spinning the plates

- Marie Kelly

'Intelligent - if she'd just apply herself' - little Marie span her plates.

'Such a waste of talent' - teen Marie tried so hard to spin her plates.

'So conscientious and hard working' - young adult Marie span her plates with ease.

'Every day is the same' - young mum Marie thought as she span her plates feeling unfulfilled.

'I love learning' - student Marie exclaimed as she contently span her plates.

'Such an achievement' - graduate Marie thought spinning her plates gleefully.

'I want to do everything so well' - Social Worker Marie span her plates.

'I'm struggling to maintain my high standards' Marie realised as the plates started to slow.

'I've let everyone down' - Marie saw her plates were barely moving.

'Doctor I feel like I have been spinning plates all my life; I can't spin them anymore'.

'Well I've always been a bit distractible could it be ADHD?' Marie thought as she started to spin her plates slowly.

'There's medication to help me spin my plates?' Marie's plates increased in speed.

'This is amazing, there's so much more time in the day!' Marie's plates span faster.

'I wish I'd known I had ADHD before, my life could have been much easier!' I spin my plates as best I can.

Being a neurodivergent Social Worker: a daily Russian Roulette

- *Hannah*

Russian roulette, will I wake up tired in the morning?
Right now, I lay awake because my thoughts are exhausting.
My brain driving at full speed through an unknown maze,
A tangled web of thoughts and worries keeping me awake.
When I do get to sleep, there's many demons in my dreams,
So vivid, my mind racing, what does it all mean?

I stumble out of bed, following my usual morning routine,

But I arrive at work later than I was meant to be.
I sit at my desk and emails start to come through,
I start to read them, forgetting what else I was meant to do
A ping comes up, I should have been in a meeting...
Now it's late afternoon, and I still haven't eaten

The chaos is expanding, there's many calls that I have missed,
I try to stay in control by writing a "to do list",
But now there's so much loud noise and my head is hurting
My brain is all jumbled and not really working.
I try to rush through, quickly replying to all the texts,
But what I have written is wrong and doesn't make sense.
Now I'm being asked questions I don't remember from last week,
I'm so tired now. I have no energy to speak.

My body feels drained, my tank running on empty,
Any motivation or desire has completely left me.
Now everyone thinks that I'm being "anti-social",

I wish I was less awkward, and someone who spoke up more,
But in the past, I have not recognised all the social cues,
people misunderstood me or thought that I was rude.
So, I've often stayed quiet, in fear of making errors,
Wondering if I'll feel like a human mess forever.

But I hope this poem helps people to be more accepting of me,
A neurodiverse Social Worker with OCD and ADHD.
I'm now learning to be kinder and truer to myself,
I know that it's OK to not be the same as everyone else,
We're all unique and different, with talents to share far and wide,
Sparkling and shining all around, lighting up the sky
There's so many of us under the neurodivergence umbrella,
And how amazing it would be... for the Social Work profession to understand us better.

Ode To My Struggle

- Sheila AM Leighton

Do you see me? Who I am?
I see you and maybe so much more, and can understand.
I see your struggles, your achievements, your wants.
I see your footsteps and where you leapt from.

But do you see me, who I am?
All my glories and where I stand
I come from angles and pathways that I understand,
and I make connections strand by strand.

For me, that means I need the facts, not just what you think I should know
but the thoughts behind that.
My brain needs the connections cos the gaps are just that!
I need to see you, and that's a fact.

Others struggle to see me for many reasons,
for I am a Woman, Black and Seasoned.
I don't suffer fools gladly, but I do understand,
that some may struggle for who I am.
For reasons, only God knows,
I find myself in places that don't know,
don't know me, the whole of me.
Not just the Woman, Black and Seasoned,
but that my seasoning is different, and for a reason.

You can't see me, the whole of me, but take some time, and you will see,
how I connect and make sense of the world,
which is filled with hopes and opportunities.
However, with that said, you will see my woes,
my struggles to connect with the world, to understand my place,
for I was once alone, not seen and out of place.

I was left to find my way,
and others struggled and would say, 'why do you do it that way?
I had no answer cos that is how it should be

For, if you could see me, my neurodiversity, you would understand I am unique and original and captured within a seasoning I struggled to hold,
but which held me.
Finch could see me and my possibilities. She could see me before me
Here I now stand and am getting stronger –
Woman, Black and Seasoned with a twist that is unapologetically just me!

You tried

- David Grimm

You told me you'd help,
That you'd do what it took.
Together we'd make it...

If only we could.

In all of your kindness,
You showed me the route
To those that could tell me,
Why my studies were shook.

As soon as I left though
And made my way through,
Swimming in trenches,
Covered and drowning
In neurological soup.

None of it helped,
I'm sorry to say,
And I feel like I failed you,
more than myself.

And I still don't know why,
But I'll continue to try,
And if I make it to clarity,
You'll be the first in my mind.

Bureaucratic Ties

- David Grimm

Bound in red,
Tape threading my sense.
Tying me down,
Unable to breathe,
Unable to think.

Everyone else is able to move
And able to close.
Study and think,
Pray, love, evolve.

So why do I feel,
That I'm stuck here alone,
What is this loss,
That dogs at my soul?

And why can no one,
Tell me what's wrong?

I ask and I try,
I scream and I cry,
But none of the help,
Seems worth the trials.

It's no one's fault,
They're bound in the red,
But it leaves me frozen,
And retired inside.

Who am I?

- Karen Gilbank

Once I didn't know
But it all made sense
The older I grow
I was so mixed up
Filled with anxiety and shame
Topping up my emotional cup
There was no one to blame
The hard times made me strong
While I navigated this pain
Whilst I searched to belong
Who knew it was my neurodivergent brain

At last I know who I am
A place I have found
Somewhere with my gang
No longer am I drowned
I'm now in my happy place
So excited and so proud
No longer hiding my face
No longer under a cloud

Lost in my own Mind

- Julie Barbor

As a child growing up feeling all alone, struggling with the day to day "norms"
Lost in my own mind, thinking where do I fit, within humankind.
Ostracized at school for being "different"
Sent to the corner to face the wall, all I had done was say "I don't know"
Why is living such a steep hill to climb?!

All I wanted was to fit in with the crowd
But not knowing why things were so hard
Isolated, not feeling fine when will life be a little more kind
Left behind, giving in, where do I go and when will it end.

Adulthood comes, still plodding through life,
Not knowing what my future will bring,
having no goals or challenges to win.
Feelings deep down of drowning within,
cannot see the light only darkness within,
words just confuse, cannot write or make sense
Lost in my own mind, thinking where do I fit, within humankind

It's a key part of me... Dyslexia

- Natalie Woodd

"She'd be bright, if she stopped the daydreams..." always said my report card.
TRYING to focus, but self-distracting as class fool, made it hard.
"Do as well as your sister, it's all that we ask".
But where was the support TO help me ACHIEVE the task?

It was the 70's and 80's where Thatcher held court,
The birth of neoliberalism, where challenges were your own to sort.
People were disposable, there was very little care.
Today has stark parallels, some with so much but refusing to share.

It wasn't until university that I looked around to see,
There were so many people doing similar things to me.
Pre-printing lecture slides and colour coding notes.
Made me realise we're all in the same sea, navigating very different boats.
A shared story over the years, adults missing the signs or perhaps we'd masked with our own fears?

Learning styles vary based on individual needs, each NAVIGATING at our own speed.
Finally able to pack away the SHAME dispelling the myth "you've only yourself to blame".
What's the journey taught me? The value of self-care. From surviving to thriving when I chose to dare.
How does this inform our practice? How can this knowledge be shared?
From a non-judgemental start point, offering person-centred care.
So, what can we serve from this neurodivergent pot? The simple answer is .... We bring a bloomin' lot!

Social Work in a Neurodiverse World

- *Rachael Duke*

Have you ever wondered; what Dyslexia looks like for me?

It feels like I'm juggling water - not one jug, not two, but three!

Word finding is a challenge when you have assessments galore...

I end up re-writing sentences – two times, three times, four!

Then we move on to the spelling, with those god-awful red lines

And the dictionary can't find the answer – no hope, oh dear, bad times!

Reading is always a laugh, as words jumble up you see

Appear they wrong in the order – makes little sense to me.

Now I often joke about my Dyslexia – as that is how I cope

But the daily struggles are real and sometimes I lose all hope!

Processing of information, memory struggles too,

I can't listen, look, and retain – it is just too much for my brain to do.

Despite all these challenges, there is a small ray of hope,

In the form of reasonable adjustments – these really support me to cope.

My confidence has risen, I CAN do the job and more....

Social work is now my oyster, as I continue to soar and soar.

ABC

- Belle Penbaligon

Why don't you get it? it's just ABC.
Ah that's exactly why it's not easy for me.
On goes my mask and tense my insides.
And then off go my thoughts that cannot decide.
Are angels white to camouflage in the clouds?
I want to interrupt and share my musing out loud.
But then again, I am the fool for not paying attention.
So, I force myself to at least look in their direction

Aww wow look, a wet spider web look how it glistens.
Damn it, I am off again, why can't I just listen?
Oh no, next question, focus write it down,
The presenter calls my name asks another question and frowns
The sharp inhale, or passive-aggressive tut
Yep, once again, I am seen as a pain in the butt.

I ask them to repeat it, 'please can you say it again'
When will they progress to support a NeuroD brain?
They know I am Dyslexic, but they don't know me
And how hard it is to focus on "Easy" ABC
B is for beach my happiest place,
Away from this competitive study race
Damn you thoughts, whom I must learn to tame
You need to focus or you will lose the game.

Does it happen to others? or only to me?
Where C, becomes E, and then morphs into a 3.
Being as easy as ABC
Is really hard for my mind in me.

The concept of Neurodiversity has been world changing, by giving us a new perspective on humanity.

- Judy Singer

ARTWORK

Sky Whale

- Clair Girvan

I painted this Sky Whale while having in mind the enormity of the impact that Autism has had on me. I didn't want to represent it as a heavy weight, as although the impact is often overwhelming and huge, maybe even a curse? I often also see my Autism symptoms as lifting me up, a gift, or dare I say a supernatural power. The girl therefore doesn't carry this beautiful beast, but takes it everywhere with her.

Bright Aliens

- Clair Girvan

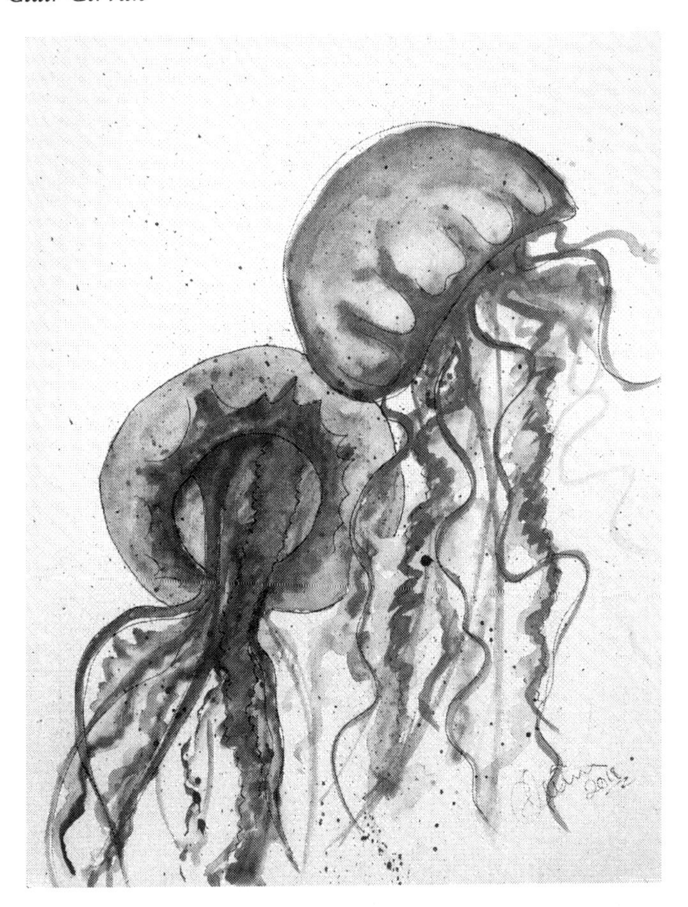

I'm often drawn towards animals that are considered weird and alien to others. I find calmness and understanding in their difference. Jelly Fish are always avoided by others, they are dangerous, unknown, weird. They are true alien creatures that still feel they shouldn't be there they shouldn't exist in their extreme difference, but gracefully navigate their environment, beautifully, changing their colours and pulses and vibrations to match their environment, I find them memorising and peaceful, they seem completely at ease with their place in the world and can explore the deepest and darkest parts of their world with grace.

Camouflage Master

- Clair Girvan

The Octopus considered a peculiar alien creature in its environment, and yet it has mastered camouflage in its environment to become hidden and unseen. It twists and squeezes its body in situations to escape danger, uses everyday things to help fade to the background ore as armour, many hands to juggle and manipulate around tasks, a quick thinker, a problem solver. People always judge an appearance and misread the skills.

Hidden Rainbow

- Clair Girvan

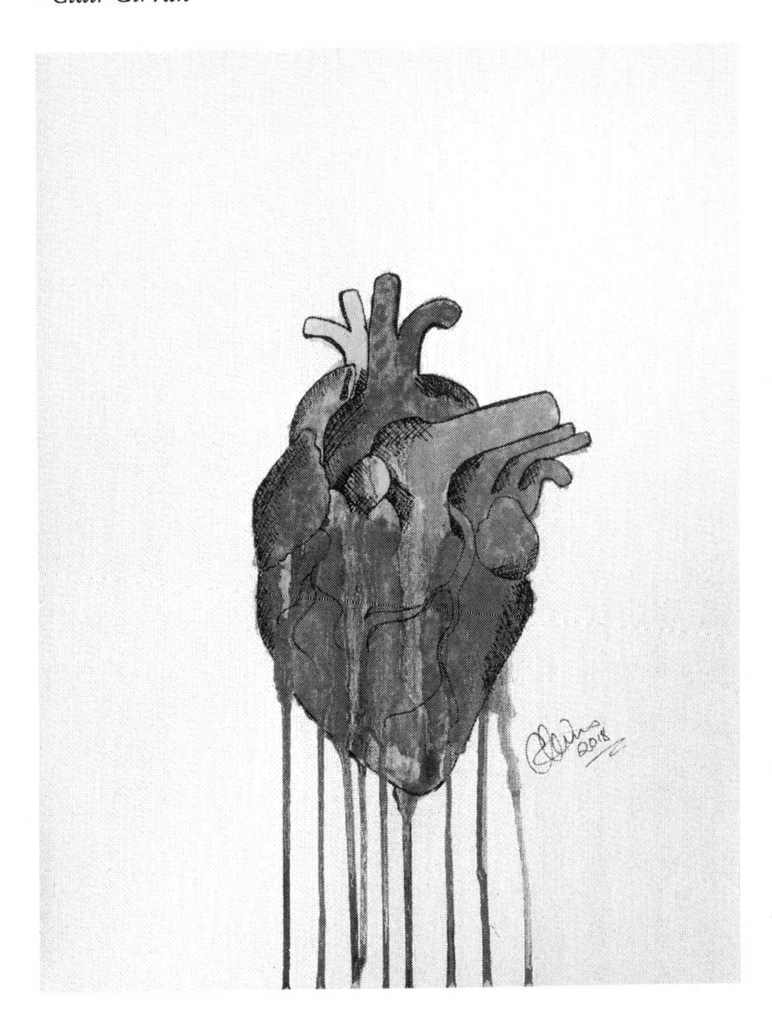

When I painted this heart, I wanted to reflect masking. Lots of people represent this by using a physical mask over the face. I wanted to reflect that masking is more than skin deep, at that at the very core the very heart the very centre of my self, is my true self, in masked and authentic. The heart is full of my colour and creativity which often feels overflowing from being muted and stifled.

Larger Than Life

- David Grimm

The flower is drawn larger than the humans, as it represents the dreams of my never-ending brain. I and many other people with neurodiverse brain types have been told throughout life that our aspirations and hopes are too large, unattainable and simply that we need to be more realistic. So, this drawing is to say that though your dreams are that of legend, you should always try to follow them, you can attain even the 'larger than life' concepts.

Drowning in Plain Sight

- David Grimm

Since being diagnosed with ADHD, lots of people have told me how they felt like people had ignored their struggling life, while they believed they were screaming for help. They described it as a suffocation / drowning, and a belief that no one would understand them ever. The woman in the picture is rising from the water because my diagnosis made me feel like I was being released from an unending current and allowed to finally breathe.

Confusion

- David Grimm

This drawing aims to show the distinction between the neurodiverse types but also the intersection of the conditions and how bewildering it can be to try and even begin to understand which condition(s) you're living with. It can be overwhelming, but you will figure it out eventually.

ARTWORK

Mosaic Minds

- Nicola Jordon

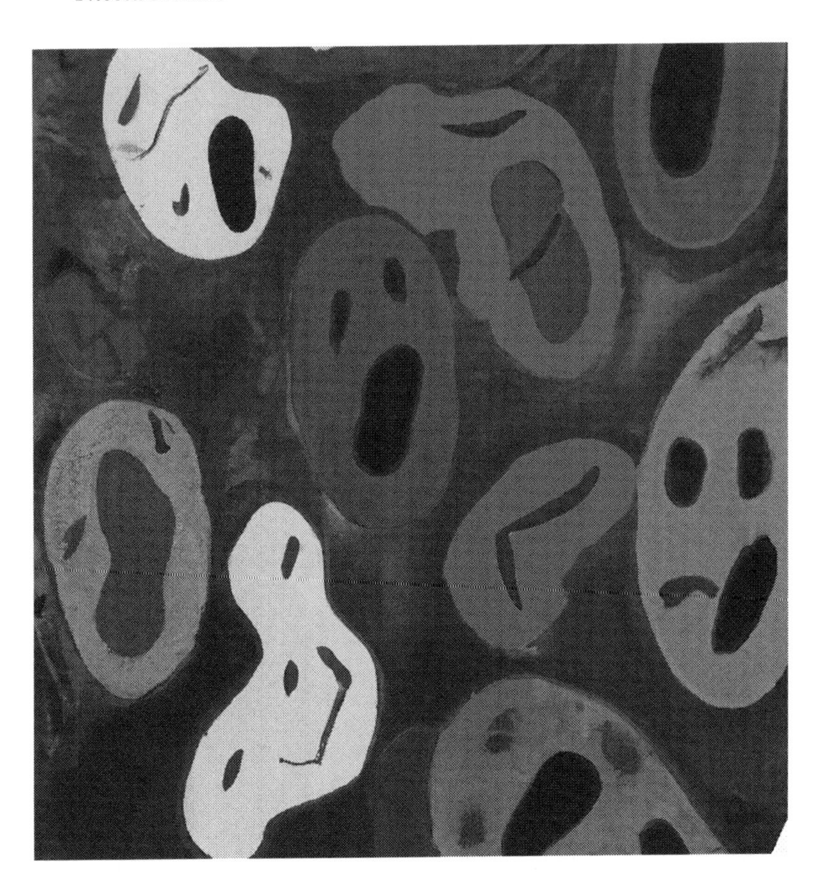

The artwork is a visual representation of the complex and multi-faceted nature of the human mind. The overlapping 'faces', each with their own unique features and expressions, come together to form a mosaic of emotions, thoughts, and experiences. The bold colours of the piece symbolise the energy and vibrancy that individuals with ADHD often possess, while the distortion of the faces represents the challenges and struggles that come with the disorder. Despite the chaos, there is a sense of harmony and unity in the overall composition, reminding us that each person's mind is a work of art, with its own unique beauty and complexity.

“Miss Understood”

- Kally Hawkins

This artwork depicts who I am as a whole; more than the sum of my parts or collection of symptoms. Any label can be misunderstood, misrepresenting us in our holistic sense, and at times I am misunderstood by others based on their assumptions. I experience a range of symptoms with ADHD, some compliment my naturally optimistic nature, whilst some are challenging. This diagnosis does not define me, it is incorporated into my other attributes and delightfully messy flaws.

The image of self is a black outline on a white background, demonstrating the body as a template. The traits and characteristics are written in colour as they give vibrancy and animation to our identity and personhood.

ARTWORK

ADVICE

Why an Advice Section?

This book is brimming with advice for neurodiverse professionals and for neurotypical people who want to be an ally and support their neurodiverse colleagues. Some contributors included advice in their reflections and others sent us separate advice. In this section we have pulled together the advice and added some of our own. We hope that it will be helpful to you. We have tried to structure the advice around the different stages in the social work journey. However, there is a great deal of crossover and so it may be useful for you to read the different sections of advice, even if it does not relate to the stage you are at in your own journey.

The following webinars also contain lots of advice:

Neurodiversity in Social Work: A Lived Experience of Difference

Guest speakers share their experiences and provide a range of advice.

Time Management: Some Advice for Social Workers

This session provides a range of advice on time management which could be useful.

Advice to my Younger Self

In this session, 99 people provide one piece of advice to their younger self. Lots of the advice could be helpful to neurodiverse practitioners.

Adult Learning Theory

This session provides some information about adult learning theory. It concludes with Nicola discussing her neurodiversity and describing her own techniques for study.

Essay Writing

This session provides a range of ideas for essay writing, drawing on diverse approaches.

What works for me might work for you!

- Pete Nevison

Neurodiversity tools, strategies and support has gradually improved over the years. In my reflection I highlighted that in the 1980/90's the world was a much different place for neurodivergent people. Technology has improved things dramatically. However, there is much more to be done both as neurodiverse people and general society in order to tackle the systems around us, this includes in and out of the workplace. It is here that I am going to go through some of the things you can do to help yourself whether you have a formal diagnosis or not.

Firstly, I paid for an educational psychologist to assess me before I came back to education to study. Colleges/Schools and some Universities are often not quick at picking this up. Workplaces as a general rule are not paying for educational psychologist assessments. The benefit of obtaining a psychologist report is that it opens doors to access support which is more difficult without a statement. Don't get me wrong, we shouldn't need a statement to get the assistance required. However, in current society this helps, especially if you are going back into education, or you are already in this flux. These reports are not cheap but are worth considering in order to provide guidance to others on what strengths you already have and also what areas are for development, support and understanding.

If you need more information on this have a look at https://www.bdadyslexia.org.uk/services/assessments/diagnostic-assessments. The British Dyslexia Association (BDA) is a great resource, and I would recommend having a good read of their website. If you don't have a diagnosis but you are considering how this might help, this is a good starting point. Employers in my view need to get better at picking this up and referring in for assessment because many people in the workplace were not picked up by the educational system. These people have never had a diagnosis and are often left to find their own way in the workplace. I would also say that if you suspect you are neurodiverse then see if your employer has some sort of disability staff network or if they sign up to the Disability Confident employer scheme https://www.gov.uk/government/collections/disability-confident-campaign. You may be able to get some advice and support reviewing these approaches and maybe you'll be able to get your employer to pay for a test, or part pay for one. Employers that support neurodiverse colleagues are better placed to utilise the person's strengths and see organisational rewards as a result. If you are employed and can verify your neurodiverse condition, just ask for what you need. Employers can refer you to Access to Work https://www.gov.uk/access-to-work but they have to fund a percentage of this cost, so if what you need is less than their contribution, just ask for the equipment or software. Access to Work often delays the length of time it takes to obtain the required support within organisational networks, like I.T. for instance, can stall this further. This has been at least my experience.

At this point you might be saying, "I don't have a statement? I can't afford to get a psychologist report? I am struggling at work but this stuff will take time....." This might be the case and I had this issue for many years before I took control. This next part is about things that you can buy off the shelf to assist you, for example, software, smartphone tech and approaches you are likely to already have at your disposal. Let's break some of this down into additional categories.

Organisation, collecting information and meeting deadlines

Smartphones made a massive impact on my ability to manage my time in work and my personal life. I will add calendar appointments, sometimes I will include my work email address so that I can add the same thing to my work Outlook calendar. I can have a family shared calendar on my smartphone. All electronically and most importantly with reminders. Yes, I set reminders to make sure I attend things. This was a nightmare before modern technology and specifically smartphones are probably the most accessible and easy way for me to be professional, on time and organised.

Outlook or other organisational calendars you are using, are your friend if you are neurodiverse. If you don't make time to organise and plan, it will cause you stress and you're likely to frustrate your employer and/or miss deadlines, thinking about education for instance and handing in assignments on time. I use my calendar as my personal accountability tool.

Spreadsheets or word tables are also a good tool to collect projects (you can create headers and columns), tasks and add any deadlines. I often write things into a notebook and get this into my database quickly whilst the notes mean something to me. If I leave it too long, I lose the meaning and urgency which catches me out at meetings. Use your calendar to block out time to think, this allows you to process actions in your working day. We all need time to think and process actions to do a good job. Back-to-back meetings are never a good idea but at times are unavoidable. Be your future friend and block out time that is for you to capture ideas, plan and for processing of tasks, hopefully from the spreadsheet or word table that provides structure. There are many productivity books out there and in audio format and I have used some of the tools and advice to get things done from these.

Creative Thinking

Getting your thoughts out can be hard at least to pull them into an organised fashion. I can still struggle with this often because I am good at problem solving but not always at testing my thinking to show people how my brain got to that outcome or proposal. If I am not careful and I do this, I can jump to solutions before I have a complete picture of the issues faced. Therefore, keeping my creative thinking and then breaking this down into follow on tasks is absolutely essential. You can physically write down mind maps and then list further follow up actions, inputting this into a database list. However, if you like to save these and keep track this can be a challenge in itself. Inspiration 10 https://www.inspiration-at.com/ is a great tool for this and if you have a report/diagnosis it should be easy to get this onto your workstation. You may be able to just ask for it as a reasonable adjustment under the Equality Act but some employers may decline this until you go through the Access to Work process. This software allows me to mind map ideas and turn those ideas into research, plans and reports. It is brilliant in my personal opinion.

Word will do some basic visual options but if you can get your employer to pay for Microsoft Visio you can process map thinking. This will allow use of the visual tools to mark out what questions you might need more information to answer. Having an ideas list with things to think about can help. Make sure you keep the digital folder locations organised and have an archive folder for historic items you don't need any more but might need to reference later.

Spelling and reading

Spell check in word is pretty good these days and if you can't remember a specific word, what I do is write another word that has similar meaning and then, right click, click 'Synonyms' and this will often find the word I am looking for. You can get software that will spell check and read your documents. If you don't have this, I find converting documents into a PDF can help because I can then listen to the large document as a PDF and I often hear spelling errors that allow me to correct this before it goes out to a wider audience. In the 365 version of word I can listen to the written work but it is much more robotic in sound. The PDF reader is specifically useful when I want to read government guidance or review policy. I often get reading fatigue so being able to use these cheats allows me to mentally bank my focus time for the work I need to produce.

I mentioned audio books earlier, I really struggle to read anything long and rapidly get tired which doesn't leave me with the ability to focus when I need too. I find audio books a really useful tool and I have listen to many books about project management, business design and getting things done. I have been able to apply some of that thinking into my strategies. I mostly use Audible but other audio book providers do exist.

Interviews and reasonable adjustments

Interviews are hard for anyone, lets face it, they are not the best experiences. However, good employers are looking to get the best fit of person into their vacancy so don't be afraid to ask for an adjustment. Interviews should not be a test, treated like an exam, they should be a conversation, but I know this will vary from company to company. I personally have poor short term working memory and companies have caught me out with time limits on questions, not sharing them ahead of an interview or not applying a time adjustment for this. Their approach when this has happened has shown 'unconscious prejudice' resulting in disadvantage at the interview. I have listened to HR podcasts and views on this subject, but I cannot reference them here because I cannot specifically remember the titles. However, what I will say is ask for your adjustments, if you can be specific then do so because if you leave it to the employer to interpret what is deemed reasonable it is likely to be undoubtedly unreasonable, because they do not know you. I know from experience that I need to ask for questions ahead of the interview (if the employer will allow this), if they won't I need to ask them to provide the questions one by one in writing as well as saying them. I have recently learnt that if I get a time allowance on an activity for my interview that I need to also ask for a time allowance on questions, especially if they are using any sort of time monitoring device. I will point out at this point that stop watching people in interviews is not good practice, in real life you can go away with questions and rely on natural pauses. Employers need to be mindful that if they have signed up to the Disability Confident Scheme, how they are making this accessible for people to get the best out of them at interview. You can rightly ask that question. Stating what you think is reasonable doesn't mean you'll get it but you need to ask because the right employer will pick up on this and make suitable adjustments to help get the best out of you.

Confidence, positivity and learning things that are new (thinking about memory)

Learning new things is hard, I am going through this at the moment as I type this, as part of my new role. I am working in a new organisation, with new processes, systems approach, demographics and resources. Be confident to say what you need, why it's important and how you will use that to benefit your role and the organisation as a whole. Use your calendar to protect your thinking time. Write things down and record them in an action plan. Use whatever tools and approaches you have found most useful as a second brain, to support your thinking, actions and learning.

Finally, thanks for reading some of my tips, thoughts and strategies. These are specific to me. It is important to say that every neurodivergent person is different. However, some of the strategies may be helpful to develop and manage things that are maybe not as controlled or as organised as you would like. There are other approaches I have developed and that are not captured here. However, I am mindful I could write a whole book on this topic, so on a parting note, thank you for taking the time to read this and hopefully it will help to think about your approach as someone neurodiverse, or as an employer or even as a colleague.

Top tips for educators

- Sam Keeton

I struggled in mainstream schooling, but was not diagnosed with anything, I was just labelled naughty/disruptive. Both of my parents were diagnosed with various neuro diversities, though I feel not necessarily the correct ones. My difficulties were first recognised in college where it was suggested I had Dyslexia (like my mother). I was formally diagnosed with "non Specific Learning Difficulties" whilst studying for my degree at university and was then supported with DSE grants and given adaptations to support my learning. Since having my daughter 6 years ago (who has many ASD and ADHD traits), I have substantially screened in for both conditions, and have been waiting on the diagnostic pathway for nearly 4 years now, as has my daughter.

The advice below was collected when I started to write the article for the book. Over the years I have been told "you have a really good way of explaining things" but until I wrote the article, I don't think I really considered how. So, I asked people, and the below was what was they responded with, as they told me I also reflected, these are the tools I use, and I'm super glad they work.

- I use different ways to convey information, I don't just direct someone to a website (though I do direct people as well) I also direct them to videos, to podcasts, to books, to real people on twitter or in real life, to fiction, to non-fiction, I use PowerPoints (or make videos of my own) with lots of colour and pictures and visual explanations, I use flow charts and walk them through step by step how to do something.

- I am methodical and this is useful for others as I break things down to the little steps others may glance over, even down to clicking an "obvious" button on screen, or where a certain thing is specifically located (not just "on the P drive.")

- I often teach in metaphor and story, so I use simple, easy to understand examples of times I or others have also done something similar. I use both times I have done well, and times I have not done well, to help others take better paths. Where something maybe hard to understand for someone NT, such as why being in a café or supermarket could be causing someone to meltdown, I give them relatable examples such as times they have walked past a building site and the power tools have been blaring yet they are trying to navigate where they are walking, or times they might have been on a night out but the music so loud and the room so dark they cannot see or hear the people around them sometimes causing a feeling of fear or panic.

- I tailor supervisions (formal and informal) to the person being supervised. I check on their wellbeing as much as their cases. I give space to talk about things that are important to them. I share strategies, but do not expect them to use them all, as what works for one doesn't always work for another. I ask if they need to dedicate more time on one thing than others so that they have extra time and space to pull apart specific things, rather than wasting time on things they feel they have a good grip on.

- I make myself available and make nobody feel that they are not worth my time. This is not to say I am not very busy and need to come back to people, but if someone needs me, or needs some space to reflect, I make space, I make time. I really listen, take my time and don't dismiss how a situation is making them feel, which gives them the confidence to accept their own limitations, but also push their comfort zones knowing I have their backs.

- I have a good balance of being there, but also giving my team the space to become autonomous. Nobody feels that they are being watched, but they also don't feel like I'm not there supporting them and guiding them to strive for better. They also feel able to come back to me over and over without judgement.

- I am relatable, I don't put myself on a pedestal or stay distant or behave as though I am better/higher. I am honest about my own needs and limitations, which helps them feel confident to be honest about their own. I readdress power and ensure everyone from the student in the team to the AP all feel their knowledge and experiences are equally as important to the team.

- I ensure they understand, and if they do not understand I try again in a different way, and then again in a different way.

- I ensure I understand before attempting to impart my knowledge to others, and where I don't, I will learn, or will join them on discovering the answer.

- I HORDE information (part of being methodical), local activities, system processes, forms etc... anything that can prove useful, and I use this to help other people learn, and where there isn't a clear easy to follow thing already for the situation, I make one, like my ever growing directory of useful information.

Your needs are as individual as you

- Kulchuma Begum

As a neurodiverse social worker some advice I would give is:

- Use the screening tool if your college or university has one. As there are many people, like me, who have struggled through education without a diagnosis. If your university does not have a screening tool but you feel there may be underlying issues ask them if they can support you in identifying if there is an issue. Most college and universities have a disability service that can assist you with this.

- Don't be afraid to try different methods to find what works for you, everyone's neurodiversity is as unique as them so what works for one may not always work for another. It's all about trial and error to find what suits you and your needs.

- Social media is a great way to meet other neurodiverse people, where you can share ideas, strategies and resources that have worked for you to support others or yourself

- Embrace your diversity and stand out from the crowd because that's what makes you, YOU!

Advice for applicants to social work

- Siobhan Maclean and Kelly Bentley-Simon

- Social work needs people like you. Go for it!
- Advise the programme that you are applying to about your neurodivergence and ask for reasonable adjustments in the application process.
- Think carefully about why you want to be a social worker. Focusing on this will be important throughout your career.
- When preparing for interviews it could be helpful to reflect on the ways that you have been oppressed because of your neurodivergence. This may help to deepen your understanding of the mechanisms of oppression which will be useful in preparing for social work which is a profession built on anti-oppressive practice.
- Identify your strengths as well as your needs and struggles. Social work education can lead to you focusing on what isn't going well and what you need to improve. Whilst this is important it can lead to a focus on self-criticism and you need to find the balance to ensure that you work on your strengths too.
- Social work is an amazing profession and a real privilege, but it can be stressful. You will need to think about your own self-care, so start to develop strategies now.

To the person reading this, I want you to know that difference doesn't equal failure. You are not 'stupid' or any other word used to bring you down. It's okay if you don't know how to spell or if you struggle with maths. Being neurodivergent isn't a weakness or a fault, and it won't stop you from achieving your goals in life.

Diana Katoto

If symptoms are having a negative impact on your life and ability to achieve what you believe yourself to be capable of, talk to someone. Whether you just find strategies to help yourself or you seek diagnosis and perhaps treatment, do something about it so you don't continue to be stuck and not fulfilling your potential.

Chris Norman

Advice for social work students

- Siobhan Maclean and Kelly Bentley-Simon

- Try to further develop your thoughts around why you want to be a social worker. Focusing on this will be important throughout your career.
- In social work training you should learn more about yourself and the way that you view the world. This means that it is not unusual for neurodivergent traits to be identified during training. Seek an assessment if it will be helpful to you.
- Be clear about your learning requirements and any reasonable adjustments you might need. Don't try to hide anything, it will come out at some point and then it will be harder to deal with.
- Communication skills are particularly important in social work. It is helpful to start the development of these skills by thinking about how you communicate your own needs. The following may be helpful with this:

  Communicating a diagnosis: "*I have Dyslexia and/or X this means I have trouble with written tasks/something else, here's a brief video/website... etc.*"

  Communicating specific needs: "*I have difficulties with attention/something else, I struggle with remembering/ understanding what you're saying/coping with loud noises etc.*"

  Communicating adaptations: "*I need you to/ it would be helpful if you could...use short sentences,/use visuals, I need a break etc.*

Communicating clarification strategies (repairing breakdowns in communication): "*Please can you...say it again/tell me what that word means/wait until I have written that down, did you mean...etc.*"

- Anticipating what support you will need on placement can be tricky – you don't know what you don't know. Ask people further on in their studies for their thoughts. What works for others might work for you.
- Rejection sensitivity can mean that neurodivergent people are more defensive when being given feedback. Make sure that you take an open approach to receiving feedback and use it as an opportunity for growth. People give you feedback because they want you to be the very best practitioner you can be.
- Don't be afraid to ask questions – your questions will also be helpful to other people.
- Spend time identifying your strengths. It's easy to be deficit based which isn't always helpful.
- Be open and proactive in your approach to learning. Be prepared.
- Find out what is available to you and make use of this. This might be practical - software, study rooms, recording devices etc or it may be adjustments - extra time, extended library loans, staggered deadlines etc. You can't arrange things instantly so plan ahead.
- Remember that the only person you should compare yourself to is you.

Self-doubt is going to happen, but try not to let it cloud the skills you have.
Self-doubt is greedy, the more you feed it, the bigger it grows... Learn to starve it and get ready to flourish.

Deb

Advice for newly qualified social workers

- Siobhan Maclean and Kelly Bentley-Simon

- Keep hold of why you want to be a social worker. This may be challenged early in your career. Hold on tight to your 'why?'

- Be clear with your employer from the outset what reasonable adjustments you will need.

- Develop skills in how and when to advocate for yourself at the right level and social context.

- You may experience a 'dip' in the early part of your career (Siobhan refers to the six-month dip). This might be a dip in motivation, a dip in confidence or a dip in energy levels, in fact it can be a dip in everything! Work with this. It happens. Talk to others about it (they will have experienced it too).

- Remember this is a transition stage – you are just starting to learn about your 'social work self.' Don't be too hard on yourself.

- Rejection sensitivity can mean that neurodivergent people are more defensive when being given feedback. Make sure that you take an open approach to receiving feedback and use it as an opportunity for growth. People give you feedback because they want you to be the very best practitioner you can be.

- Siobhan finds that early in peoples' careers they often take things more personally. That difficult telephone conversation, that challenge from the person you are working with... Rejection sensitivity may mean that neurodivergent practitioners will take things even more personally and they may find it more difficult to move on from a challenging conversation. Put some work into this because it is likely to be an issue for you throughout your career.

- Connecting with others is important. Look for and join any groups or networks that might provide support. Many organisations and workplaces have special interest groups.

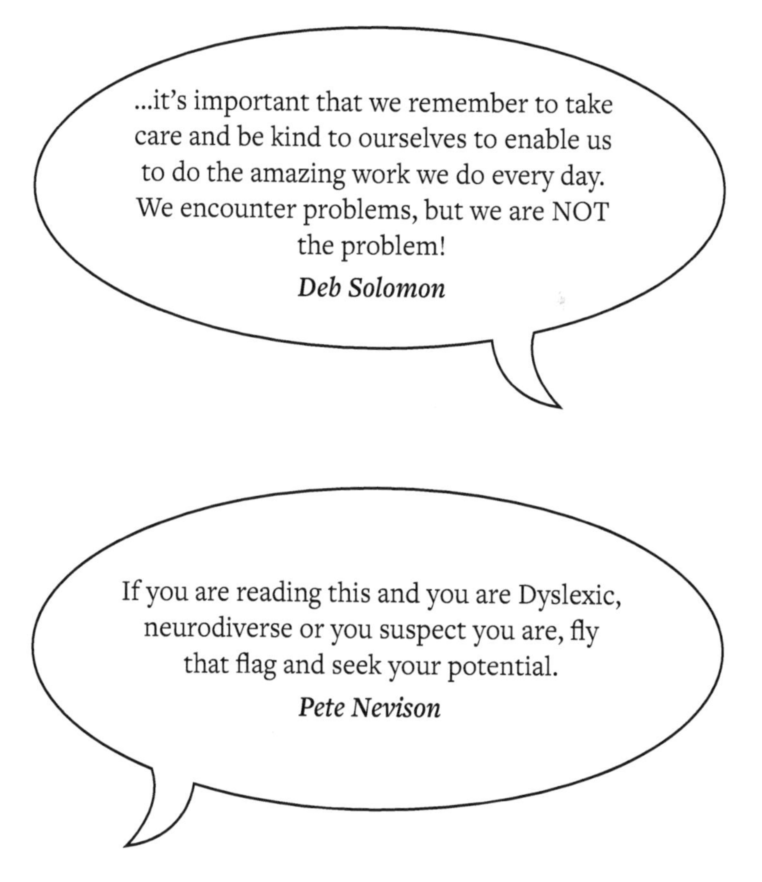

Advice for practice educators

- Siobhan Maclean and Kelly Bentley-Simon

- If you are neurodivergent then consider letting students know. Understanding your learning style can help them to think more about their own approach to learning and consider inclusivity more fully. It is also important for everyone to see neurodivergent role models in social work.

- Ask students why they want to be a social worker. Help them to develop their thoughts about this in more depth as it will be important for them to focus on this throughout their career.

- Sometimes the early stages of a placement can be deskilling for students because the focus is often on what they *can't* do. Ask students about their learning needs and any specific requirements that they have but also talk to them about their strengths and take care to build on these.

- Rejection sensitivity can mean that neurodivergent people are defensive when being given feedback. Make sure that the feedback you provide is consistently constructive. It can also be helpful to provide a very concrete evidence base for your feedback. Siobhan finds that the SBI feedback technique can be particularly helpful when working with some students. This involves outlining the situation (S), the behaviour (B) and the impact of this behaviour (I) you can also add an alternative behaviour and speculate on the alternative impact. This can be helpful in supporting people to think more fully about the impact of their behaviours.

- Siobhan often finds that the 'need to know motivation' in adult learning is particularly important in working with neurodivergent students. Ensure that the student understands why they need to know something or why it is important that they develop their skills in a particular area.
- Remember that every learner is unique. What works for one student may not work for another.
- Don't compare students.

I wish my practice educator took the time to learn about Dyslexia and Dyspraxia, to reflect on the ways our brains might differ and how differences impact the way we think/do. Most of all, I wish she and I were kinder to myself.

Florence Smith

Advice for University lecturers / tutors

- Siobhan Maclean and Kelly Bentley-Simon

- If you are neurodivergent then be as open as you can about this. It is important for students to see positive role models in their education.
- Make learning a collaborative process. Flip the learning too – we are all educators and we are all learners.
- Find out what your students already know about social work. Some students know more than others and peer learning is particularly useful when supporting neurodivergent students.
- Consider the starting point of your students, these will all be different and our experiences, including those of neurodivergence mean we each see the world differently.
- Be informed about your students, familiarise yourself with any important information that could affect their ability to attend, participate and learn in your lessons.
- Kelly feels it is particularly important that lecturers make themselves available to students. Be approachable, students need to feel they can talk to you, neurodivergent students particularly may struggle to see that you want to help.
- Try to give an outline of the structure and timings of the session at the start. Being clear about breaks can be helpful to people. It is important to remember that this can change but even a flexible structure is better than no structure.

- Use different techniques in your teaching. Different brains need different learning styles. A mixture of speaking, group work, slides etc well ensure more of what you teach is retained.

- Kelly says that one of the most memorable modules for her was one where the lecturer provided a recap of the previous session by asking students what they remembered and then filling in the gaps. This along with a brief explanation at the start and recap of the session at the end will ensure your students have the best chance of being able to recall their learning.

- After teaching complex topics, ask your students to explain what they have learnt to someone else, doing this means that they have to synthesise the information into its simplest form.

- Be aware of and try to limit any distractions in your classroom / lecture hall, taking into account sensory differences. Be mindful of allowing people to choose where they sit, they may need to avoid noise from the corridor or move away from bright lights or other things that may cause distractions.

- Clarify which items on your module list are essential and which are for further reading. A large reading list can be overwhelming and some students will need a little direction as they may think they need to read everything.

- Where possible, show examples of work, Kelly says that seeing examples of work that passed and work that didn't, and noticing the differences helped her to understand what a "good" piece of work looked like.

- Remember that, as always, there are no one-size-fits-all strategies. All neurodivergent people are different and will have variable strengths, and support needs. The best person to tell you what a neurodivergent student needs, is that person!

Advice for trainers

- Siobhan Maclean and Kelly Bentley-Simon

- If you are a neurodiverse trainer, then consider sharing this, as it can help others to talk about their own style and needs. As a trainer you are in a position of power and to some extent you may be a role model to others. Identifying your own style can therefore be empowering for people.

- Make sure that in your planning you look out for any access requirements or specific needs. Wherever you can try to address these.

- Kelly feels one of the most common adjustments is access to presentation slides before a session. This doesn't need to be the full presentation and content, a brief bullet point list that includes long references and quotes can be a useful 'skeleton' for a person to build their own notes around.

- Allow participants to communicate with you privately before or during the session to communicate their support needs.

- Recognise that every learner is unique. In any slides or activities draw on different thinking styles – use visual as well as verbal techniques.

- Remain curious and open to peoples' needs and experiences of the training. This models the importance of professional curiosity in social work.

- Be open to learning about what you could do to be more inclusive of different neurotypes in your training.

- Try to give an outline of the structure and timings of the session at the start. Being clear about breaks can be helpful to people. It is important to remember that this can change but even a flexible structure is better than no structure.

- Ask specifically for feedback from people about how neuro-inclusive they think the experience of training was – this will also encourage neurotypical people to think about inclusivity.

- If delivering training online, allow a person to turn their camera and mic off for a short while if they need to do this. For some people who struggle with attention levels, this may boost their ability to pay attention and stay engaged.

- Siobhan feels where training face to face it can be helpful to put things on the tables – card sets, sensory items (small things to fiddle with / doodle on). It can make the room more inviting but be careful to avoid sensory overload. Kelly feels when she has attended training where thought like this has been put into the environment it has enhanced her engagement and concentration and she has been more likely to remember the content of the training.

> Review policies and procedures to ensure that they are Neurodiverse inclusive. Openly catering for those with Neurodiverse traits in training... will benefit all employees but, more importantly it will be bringing Neurodiverse traits into the open, encouraging conversations, connections and increasing acceptance and inclusivity, positively impacting on the working environment and culture for all.
>
> *Sandy Symonds*

Advice for team managers

- Siobhan Maclean and Kelly Bentley-Simon

- If you are neurodivergent, consider telling your team. You are a role model. Promote discussion about what this might mean and encourage conversation about diversity within the team. This can enhance psychological safety for everyone in the workplace.

- Talk to team members about why they became a social worker and help them to keep focused on this in their work.

- Recognise that every social worker brings something unique to the team. Help every team member to think about what they bring.

- There is a great deal of value in buddying. Neurodivergent social workers and neurotypical social workers could make good buddies for one another as each will bring their strengths to the critical friendship. Consider how this might work in your team.

- Consider every team member's individual needs and ensure that they have appropriate support and opportunities.

- Think about how best to adapt supervision for each workers' individual needs. Good quality reflective, emotionally supportive supervision is essential for everyone. What works for one person may not work for another.

Interviewers and employers can be inclusive and champion their disability confident schemes by taking some time to think and check in with the person. They can provide materials ahead of meetings, training, or interviews. If there's a timed element to allow for the working memory and processing speeds, in real life there are natural pauses, or you can take questions away.

Pete Nevison

Advice for anyone who wants to be an ally

- Siobhan Maclean and Kelly Bentley-Simon

- Be kind.
- Be curious.
- Advocate for your neurodivergent colleagues.

...try not to see a diagnosis as 'just a label'. Because for some of us, it's a label that could change our support and life. It can validate our experiences and give explanation to why we may do things differently... bring understanding and give rise to our neurological strengths.

Florence Smith

...if you know that person that may come across as anti-social or interrupt your conversations or want to do something a certain way, be curious about why that might be. Always ask why and then repeat again and again.

Karen Gilbank

We need to ask ourselves how we react and support people with brains that are neuro-diverse and how inclusive social work is. A good starting point would be to question our own knowledge .... and...assumptions. We need to embrace the strengths and possibilities that neurodiversity can bring to social work.

Caroline Aldridge

It doesn't matter if someone has a formal diagnosis of a particular condition or not. If they can recognise themselves as having neurodiverse traits, then it is about supporting that person to meet the goals that they are aiming for. We need to remember that the process of diagnosis itself is challenging and can carry an emotional cost... Gaining a diagnosis should be a personal choice. It can be helpful in discovering particular traits and once having that knowledge being able to go on to find strategies and/or technology that helps to maximise skills and abilities.

Sandy Symonds

AUTHORS

About the Authors

- *Aga M. Buckley*

Aga M. Buckley wears colourful clothes and keeps too many books and plants, she misunderstands work for play and colour-codes her diary. Her love for learning, meaningful relationships and acceptance is fuelled by the experience of different cultures, human diversity, and years of direct mental health practice. Passionate about creativity, Aga advocates for equity, seeking to question and often contest uniformity in her personal life, education, and social work practice.

She qualified as a social worker in 1999 with a Diploma in Social Work and a degree in Social Pedagogy and worked in various roles within health organisations and local authorities. She used social pedagogic ethos in her social work practice while specialising in mental health over the years. During that time, she completed Master's in Advanced Mental Health Practice, which supported her work as an Approved Mental Health Professional (AMHP) and Best Interests Assessor (BIA). She also worked as Practice Lead and Principal Social Worker (PSW), implementing the Assessed and Supported Year in Employment (ASYE) in different local authorities before she transitioned to her current academic role.

She initially joined Kingston University's Department of Social Work and Social Care as Honorary Senior Lecturer while continuing in direct social work. Later leading modules across postgraduate and undergraduate courses, teaching social work theory, legislation, applied social work practice and social pedagogy. Her current doctoral research much inspired by background in mental health, explores lived experience of compassion fatigue among early career social workers.

Aga is a lifelong learner, as a Senior Fellow of the Higher Education Academy (SFHEA) she remains a keen supporter of interprofessional and multidisciplinary teaching and learning. She continues exploring alternative ways students and staff learn from each other, and from other disciplines. She is seconded to the Academic Staff Development in the University's Learning and Teaching Enhancement Centre where she works with academic staff across different faculties. As a registered social worker she is an active member of the British Association of Social Workers (BASW): Neurodivergent Social Workers Special Interest Group and Equality, Diversity, and Inclusion (EDI) Advisory Group. She also supports the Kingston University's Network of Equality Champions, Faculty's EDI Action Group and Social Justice and Inclusion Special Interests Group.

Born on the Baltic Sea coast in Gdansk, Aga not so secretly credits her family and love for her journeys and mixed cultural identity. She travelled and lived in various countries across the world over the years, before settling in London. She lives with her husband in the 'family of hedgehogs' as she lovingly refers to their 'spiky profiles', their cat Lynx and Ruby the snake.

Shout out - To Gary for his love, patience, and never understood sense of humor & our children for relentlessly teaching us new ways!

Linkedin: Aga M. Buckley

Twitter: @AgaMB2

- Amanda P.

Amanda has an undergraduate degree in religious studies with psychology and a masters degree in counselling psychology studies.

She returned to education in 2022 and is currently studying for an integrated masters degree in mental health nursing and social work.

Amanda has previously written articles about therapeutic writing, and had two monologues about mental health performed.

Shout out - Thank you to everyone who has been patient with me, especially my family.

Thank you also to the people who kept believing in me, even when I didn't.

- *Belle Penhaligon*

Belle Penhaligon, has just completed her Social Work Apprenticeship, and is due to start on her ASYE later this year. Belle is at the start of her Neurodiverse journey, with support from a tutor and practice educator in her final year of study to get a diagnosis.

Belle is a keen advocate for inclusion and support, especially in the workplace for people who are not neurotypical.

Belle's strengths, are empathy, seeing the unseen, problem solving and big picture logical thinking. Belle's hobbies include spending lots of time on the beach with her two daughters, and little dog Monty.

Belle has found writing poems, a great way to help re-focus her mind, when embarking on long written tasks that can be overwhelming.

Shout out - Thank you to my tutor Anna, my Practice Educator Bev, my two little Divas, my ever-supportive Mum and Dad and my wee dog Monty. Plus an extra sparkly thank you to Florence who has been a great inspiration and support.

- *Caroline Aldridge*

Caroline is a social worker, educator, author and activist. Through her work as an independent trainer and speaker, Caroline weaves together her personal and professional knowledge and experiences to promote good practice. She was a carer for her son, Tim, who had bipolar disorder and died in 2014. Her books, He Died Waiting: Learning the Lessons - a Bereaved Mother's View of Mental Health Services (2020) and They Died Waiting: The Crisis in Mental Health Services - Stories of Loss and Stories of Hope (2023) which she co-edited with Emma Corlett, articulate the experiences of people with mental illness, their carers, and families. She advocates for improved mental health services and support for bereaved relatives.

Caroline's qualifications include: Social Work BA (First Class Hons), Advanced Social Work MA (distinction), Diploma in Education and Training, and Fellow of the Higher Education Academy. She has over 30 years experience of working with children and families in a range of settings and lecturing experience includes social work, mental health and social care programmes.

Website: learningsocialworker.com
Twitter: @CarolineAldrid5
Instagram: @hediedwaiting

- Chris Norman

Chris is a social worker, working mainly with older adults for a local authority in the south of England. Having taken a range of jobs in earlier life, including everything ranging from child-minding and early years education, to teaching assistant roles, to administration, to buying wire and managing health and safety for a spring manufacturer, Chris found social work somewhat by accident having taken the first job available following a family relocation, which happened to be as administrator for the social work team where she still works, more than 10 years later.

Chris is a people person and studied Social Work independently, alongside her full-time work and family commitments. Chris graduated in 2020 during the Covid pandemic and is proud of how her practice developed through the years of learning. Chris has since begun studying for the BIA and Practice Educator qualifications and is also undertaking an MSc in Psychology to extend her learning.

Neurodivergence isn't something that Chris ever considered relevant to her life but traits spotted by friends with that experience have forced her to now consider this a potential part of her life.

Chris loves to learn and also has a keen interest in food, cooking and nutrition, having undertaken other learning in these fields to become a qualified nutritionist.

Shout out - Sincere thanks go to Kelly and David who have both caused me to think more closely about neurodivergence which resulted in my submission to this book.

Love and thanks also to my children, particularly my eldest, who has also been instrumental in me thinking about ADHD in particular.

Finally, thank you to Siobhan for your support and belief in me, and for taking me outside my comfort zone, and into new realms of opportunity.

Twitter: @chrisnorman888
Linkedin: Chris Norman

- Clair Girvan

I have loved creating since an early age, it's the time I feel most free to express myself, without judgement. Art is subjective, there is no right or wrong, there are no hard and fast rules, anyone can create art which makes it such a magical way of expressing yourself. Its my safe place.

Shout out - I would like to say a huge thank you to my boys, my husband Duncan and sons Conor and Freddie, for your love and encouragement and inspiration, love you always.

Instagram: neurospicy_artist
Etsy: neurospicyartist.etsy.com

- David Grimm

David Grimm is a social work student with experience of foster care, kinship care, residential care and the impact of being under the supportive efforts of multiple social workers. He is also a poet and artist, with most of his efforts aiming towards poetry as he finds it therapeutic and diverse as a creative art form. After he qualifies, David hopes to work alongside unaccompanied children and support them in either: returning to their families or setting up a new life that finds the children thriving as much as possible. He also hopes to study social work in other countries in order to better understand care experience as it stands throughout the world as opposed to the local knowledge that he currently holds. This of course all depends on David achieving his qualifications and becoming a practicing social worker but he feels very confident that with the support and love of his current friend group and colleagues, he can pass with no issues, ready and able to be a practical and wholesome support to those he works with.

David has recently been diagnosed with ADHD (mixed type) and has found the support from the neurodiverse community and friends to be overwhelmingly healing and believes it has been a step towards moving his life forward and empowering his future career choices.

Shout out - I would like to give a special mention to Judy Furnivall, the entire social work student connect team as well as the incredible editors of this book, Siobhan and Kelly, without the encouragement and support of these people I believe I would have continued to dwell in denial and would have suffered onwards without a diagnosis or help. With the support of the above people, I have managed to achieve some peace and mental quiet for the first time in at least 25 years of a very chaotic life.

It is and always has been my belief that I wouldn't have made it through the covid years of university without the support and encouragement of these individuals (as well as many more) and a particular gratitude for bearing with me through my more stubborn and self-sabotaging years. Thank you beyond words. I can't wait to continue being your friend and colleague once I'm a qualified practitioner.

I would love to give an enormous thanks to Siobhan and Kelly for every effort that has gone into this book, from intention to production, this book is undoubtedly a fantastic tool that will allow social workers to better understand the complex world of neurodivergence in social work... I am so grateful for champions such as yourself being in the social work world.

I am and will forever be, indescribably grateful to know you and be your friend x

Twitter: @davethecarebear

- Deb

Deb is a 50 year old Mother of 2, grandmother of 6 and wife of one.

Currently working as a children and young people social worker, and loving every day.

Deb completed a Youth Work Youth Studies degree at Teesside in 2011 and then swiftly moved on to study for a PGCE, which led her to teach Access to Youth Work and Health and Social Care in Middlesbrough. In 2019 Deb moved into Social Work, and completed a Step Up to Social Work diploma with Manchester Metropolitan University.

Deb currently supports newly qualified social workers as a 'Dyslexia Champion,' a role that helps newcomers manoeuvre their way around the service, whilst offering tips and tools to use Dyslexia as a "super power" and not a barrier.

Shout out - My Husband Marc, for his patience and time spent supporting me move forward

- *Deb Solomon*

Deb is a Social Worker within Adult Care and a practice development lead. Deb is mum to two neurodivergent teenagers and a very neurodivergent cat. After a surprise diagnosis of ADHD during the Covid lockdown in 2020 Deb set up and became Chair of the UK wide BASW Neurodivergent Social Workers Special Interest Group, which also led to becoming the Vice Chair of the BASW Equality, Diversity and Inclusion Advisory Group. The Special Interest Group meets monthly and is focused on providing peer support, as well as working on various projects including the "Celebrating Neurodivergent Social Workers" campaign; producing working guidance on supporting the neurodivergent social work workforce, and creating training through the British Association of Social Workers.

Deb is an independent trainer, providing inclusive workshops focusing on understanding neurodiversity in a range of different contexts. Her particular interests are supporting Practice Educators to support neurodivergent students, how to consider neurodiversity within safeguarding, and understanding and recognising intersectionality through a neurodivergent lens.

Shout out - Helen Jones, who at the time of my diagnosis was the Director of Adult Care within my local authority. She reached out to me, listened to me, and inspired me to be my authentic self and continue to advocate for change within the profession to promote inclusivity.

Twitter: @ND_SWgroup

Linkedin: deb-solomon-ndsocial-worker

Facebook: Neurodivergent social workers group

- Diana Katoto

Diana Katoto is a newly qualified social worker in the West Midlands, who wants to make a difference in one person's life by trying her best to advocate for the families she works with.

- Florence Smith

Florence is a qualified Dyslexic and Dyspraxic social worker. She is currently working with children and young people in the voluntary sector as a Sexual Behaviours Worker.

Florence is also an independent trainer and hosts the website and blog The Neurodivergent Social Worker - where she writes to both neurodivergent social workers and social work employers. Florence's training and writing focusses on increasing understanding of different neuro-types, facilitating psychological safety in social work and advocating for system changes to embed a neuro-inclusive culture in social work.

Florence has additionally led a campaign which celebrates neurodivergent social workers by exploring how our brains and neurological profiles support our practice whilst also exploring good practice from social work employers.

Shout out - I would like to acknowledge: Nicole for helping me change the lens in which I view my Dyslexic brain, for her commitment to neuro-inclusion in higher education (social work) and for her continued nurturing friendship; Kerry for making me feel so psychologically safe that I could begin to navigate being a Dyslexic social worker, enthusiastically, with a neurodivergent ally; Deb for creating a space and community we all needed; and everyone who has picked up this book to take accountability for understanding the experiences of neurodivergent social workers and beginning the journey to facilitate/embed neuro-inclusion.

Twitter: @flossysworld
Website: ndsocialworker.wixsite.com/ndsw
Linkedin: linkedin.com/in/florence-smith-452033247

- Hannah

My name is Hannah. I have been registered as a Social Worker since July 2021 working in childrens services.

I live by the Seaside with my partner.

I've always felt that my brain has worked differently to others and understanding who I am and my neurodivergence is an ongoing learning process. It has been great to meet other Social Workers on a similar journey and I'm looking forward to reading more of their stories in this book.

- Jenni Guthrie

I am an Autistic and ADHD social worker currently working as a Principal Curriculum Lead in a social work Masters programme as well as an independent writer, researcher and trainer focusing on Neurodivergence and social work. I am privileged to be a parent to 3 multiply neurodivergent young people and a trustee of the charity Autistic Parents UK. My passions are social justice, Scotland (I'm a proud Scot!), swimming and elephants.

Shout out - To all the Neurodivergent social workers and social work students out there, to my family and to my allied accomplices and agitators thank you; I need you, social work needs you. Keep amplifying those ND voices!

Linkedin: Jenni McCabe
Website: autisticsocialworker.co.uk

- Julie Barbor

Julie Barbor was born in Mirfield in July 1967 the younger of two children. It took a while for Julie to realise her professional passion and path in life. Mainly due to lacking interest in academia, as she had struggled at school to fit in and failed to achieve good grades. Her interest was in sports, football in particular, which used to get her in trouble at school. As it was the 70's teachers would ostracize her for playing football with the boys in break time. It was deemed not to be an appropriate activity for a girl in those days!! Consequently, Julie was judged by her teachers and peers to be troublesome as she did not conform to the "norms" expected of her as a young female. She left school at 16yrs and went from job to job, with no focus or expectations of society. Her escapism as a child / young adult growing up in the late 70's/80's facing challenges of an oppressive society and experiencing discrimination, was putting pen to paper and writing poems.

In her late 30's/40's Julie decided she wanted to become a social worker. She was successful in attaining a place at the University of Huddersfield in 2012. In her first year at university, her tutors noticed certain mannerisms and reoccurring traits in her written academic work and suggested Julie undergo a psychological test. Following this test Julie was diagnosed with having learning difficulties, Dyslexia and Dyspraxia. Nevertheless, with the additional disability support given to her and hard work, Julie went on to achieve a BSc 1st class Hons Degree in Social Work and graduated from the University of Huddersfield in 2015.

Julie now lives in Wakefield with her amazing wife, Sandii and 2 cats (Missie Moon & Salem). In her spare time, she is an ambassador for Neurodiversity Awareness and LGBTQ+ rights, previously involved on the committee for Wakefield Pride.

In 2020/2021 Julie continued in her academic goals and successfully attained a PGDip as an Approved Mental Health Professional (AMHP) at the University of Bradford. Julie is now an experienced Neurodiverse Social Worker, AMHP and Practice Educator working for Bradford Metropolitan District Council (City of Culture 2025) since 2015. Julie is currently involved in her organisations RESPECT campaign and is a proud ally, promoting the Working Together for an Inclusive Workforce ethos. Another of Julie's passions is travelling with her wife, Sandii to different countries as they both enjoy experiencing and learning about different and diverse cultures.

- Kally Hawkins

I have worked in the Health and Social Care sector for approximately 15 years qualifying as a Social Worker in 2020. Completed an undergraduate degree in Health and Social Care with the Open University.

Working at Midlands Partnership University NHS Foundation Trust allowed me continue developing myself in Social Care and to link in with Think Ahead to complete my Masters Degree in Social Work, primarily focusing on Mental Health. This was an area of interest for me as I also experience challenges with my own mental wellbeing, including depression and anxiety. I believe some of these are rooted in my neurodiversity and my experiences over the years. Working in my current team has been the first time I've really felt accepted and I don't feel like I'm constantly self-critiquing. I believe that to be a combination of the lovely people I work with, but also I believe the nature of Social Workers is to be more accepting of diversity.

I am currently undergoing my Advanced Mental Health Practitioner post-graduate certificate training and I eventually hope to become a Practice Educator and achieve my PhD.

I live with my partner and my many pets. My nieces and nephews refer to it as Aunty Kally's zoo! I've always had an interest in animals and petcare. All my (7) pets are rescued. Most of them are considered exotic pets.

Shout out - All my lovely colleagues who are very supportive and accepting; MPFT for their continued support in my development and seeing past a label to my skills; I would also like to thank Think Ahead who helped me qualify in this amazing role and have also continued to develop me and offer wider opportunities.

Twitter: Kally_Hawk

Linkedin: Kally Hawkins

Instragram/Facebook: Kally-Gary Hawkins (my nieces/ nephews can't say Kally and call me Aunty Gary)

- Karen Gilbank

My name is Karen Gilbank, I am an Advanced Practitioner Lead Social Worker at the Bradford District Care Foundation Trust (BDCFT) where I have been employed for the last 5 and a half years.

I qualified as a Social Worker in 2013 and my first qualified role was at a Local Authority working with children and young people in care. I have been employed by BDCFT since 2017, initially as a Mental Health Practitioner, then a Team Leader, I have been in my current role since February 2022. I am a Practice Educator and have lots of experience supporting students. In my main role I support social work students, apprentices, and newly qualified social workers with their Assessed and Supported Year in Employment.

Most of my work covers child and adult mental health within the community. Additionally, I work as a Mental Health Practitioner and offer clinic appointments on weekends and evenings as well as occasional shifts for our 24-hour mental health support service.

I was diagnosed with Autism and ADHD in 2021/22 which was a validating experience. I am passionate about my work and encouraging Social Workers to practice with kindness, empathy, and professional curiosity. In a world where lots of terrible things happen this is the least, we can offer.

"Wherever there is a human being, there is an opportunity for a kindness" (**Seneca**)

Shout out - A big thanks to Kelly Bentley-Simon who has been very supportive in guiding me in this process.

Twitter: @BDCFTSOCIALWORK, @Karen_gilbank

- *Karen Rodgers*

Karen qualified as a Social Worker in the UK in 2003 and practiced in Adult Services.

Karen has a strong interest in practice education and since 2006 has supported many students on placement. Since that time, Karen has built her career in various educational roles within Local Authorities, from Mental Capacity Act Coordinator, Adult Safeguarding Training Manager, Social Worker Educator and then as a Senior Lecturer in Practice Learning at Anglia Ruskin University. Karen lives on the outskirts of Cambridge, with her Working Cocker Spaniel, Bay.

Karen has become increasingly interested in neurodivergence, due to her own journey. Increasing awareness, support and valuing the strengths of people is something she feels passionate about.

Shout out - Sarah Gawne and Lee Taylor, my past and current Line Managers for their person-centered approach to me, 'being me', during my 'times of overwhelm' (code for meltdowns!)

- Kathryn Chorley

I am currently a Social Worker employed BDCFT NHS Trust as a Mental Health Practitioner and Practice Educator within the Neurodevelopmental Team at CAMHS.

The Neurodevelopmental Team specialise in assessment and diagnosis of Autism and ADHD and as a neurodiverse Social Worker myself, it is a privilege to work in this specialist area.

I think that my blend of personal and professional knowledge is so helpful in understanding the perspectives of the children and families that I work with.

It is also a privilege to work as a Practice Educator, as I think it's important to pass on good working practice and our valuable experience to the next generation of social workers.

Before joining the Neurodevelopmental Team I worked for 5 years within a Primary Mental Health Team at CAMHS, and before that I spent many years employed by the local council as a Child Protection Social Worker.

Let's not count years please ...

Shout out - Thanks to Kelly for encouraging me to get my neuro assessments.

Thanks to my Jess, Darren, Maureen and my family and friends who have loyally helped me along the way.

- *Katie Küken*

I have been a lecturer practitioner at Anglia Ruskin University since February 2021, teaching on the Social Work Apprenticeship, Undergraduate, Masters and CPD programs, and am currently training as a Practice Educator alongside this role. I was a community Mental Health Social Worker, working in various NHS mental health trusts, and an Approved Mental Health Professional.

Shout out - To Kev, Dawnie, and Reggie, for their never-ending support... and for loving me on my most difficult days.

To Jenny Rafter and Kay Aaronricks for their inspiring leadership, and for creating a safe workplace which allows us all to flourish.

To Laura Scott, for her passion for safe and supportive spaces for social workers.

To my social work colleagues who cared about my wellbeing first and foremost.

@katiekuken

- Kelly Bentley-Simon

Kelly lives in West Yorkshire with her wife, two small children and two cats. When not working Kelly can usually be found practicing a new skill, this could be learning to juggle, playing the drums or editing a book. Kelly doesn't like to be bored and often wonders why she is often tired.

Kelly is originally from Manchester (the greatest city in the world) and has lived in West Yorkshire for over 20 years, half of this time with her wife Faye.

Shout out - Thank you to Faye for your patience, keeping me fed and watered, and for supporting me to be the best version of me I can.

Thanks to my little sister Leah, for your encouragement and always going along with my crazy schemes and your encouragement.

Thanks to my work colleagues Kathryn, Karen and Vicky for your continued support.

Thank you to Siobhan for your friendship and for making this whole project possible.

Twitter: @Kelly_BFD

- Kennith Roulston

My name is Kennith Roulston I am from Glasgow and I am currently a social work student from the University of the West of Scotland Paisley. I am a third-year student with a learning disability which has been at times debilitating but also heightened through the pandemic and during lockdown. I have found writing this piece has given me an outlet to self-reflect on my experiences during the covid pandemic.

Shout out - Sarah Anderson, Simon Gittins, Paula Gow, John Sturgeon

- Kulchuma Begum

I was born in 1985 in Bangladesh, the 3rd of 5 siblings. Education was never given much importance in our family and so I left academia at the age of 17 with 5 GCSEs and returned to education after a long gap, graduating in 2022 with a BA Hons in Social Work.

I knew from a young age my calling was to work with children in some way shape or form and so after school and college I started my journey working with children from birth to 16 years old as a nursery nurse, teaching assistant and then a family support worker where my interest in social work was enhanced. I am now currently completing my Assessed and Supported Year in Employment as a School Social Worker.

I aspire to continue to work in this challenging yet rewarding field and hope to one day be able to teach in the field of social work as a lecturer which I know requires more studying, but I feel that this is definitely doable with this newfound confidence in my academic abilities.

I love food whether I'm cooking it or eating it to help me de-stress (definitely enjoy the latter a little more!). Being a busy mum of two energetic boys I enjoy the quieter moments reading and relaxing or watching a movie. I have always been one for the simplistic things and find happiness in the smallest of things which has helped me to be grateful for all I have.

Shout out - I am at a point in my life where I NEVER thought I would be, and this is only possible first and foremost because of my Husband who believed in my capabilities and supported me in any way he could to help me achieve what I have despite the older generation frowning upon my return to education. Secondly my children, my niece and my sisters who gave me the boost in morale and confidence each time the I was ready to give up. Thank you all for never giving up and me and believing in me when I didn't believe in myself.

I would also like to say a huge thank you to Siobhan Maclean and Kelly Bentley-Simon for this amazing opportunity to share my story which I hope will help others to see there is light at the end of the tunnel.

Twitter: @Kulchuma2

- *Marie Kelly*

I have always been interested in supporting people and feel rewarded by helping others achieve their goals. Social Work as a profession was something I had an interest in and always felt strongly about promoting social change. Growing up in in a very deprived area of Bristol gave me lived experience of the barriers and challenges people can encounter; sometimes bringing them to the attention of social care. These early insights were a catalyst for me to achieve more than was ever expected of me.

Although I was thought to be 'bright' from a young age, with the potential to achieve academically, I failed to convert that potential into positive results initially. Later returning to study GCSE's and an Access to Social Work course where I was able to excel.

I was the first person in my family to go to university, which was an achievement in itself, but qualifying as a Social Worker has been one of my greatest achievements so far, second to being a mother of two children. Being a Social Worker has proven to be challenging, it has continuously pushed me to develop my practice and knowledge base. Being diagnosed with ADHD was a defining moment in my career at the age of 36. I always knew deep down I might have ADHD, from being sat in the corner to avoid distraction or being known as the chatterbox of the office, the clues were always there.

In my career (prior to diagnosis) I have worked mainly in child protection and safeguarding, this area of work suited me the most. I have a natural ability to connect with people, particularly those deemed 'hard to engage', the more challenging the situation, the more rewarding I find a positive outcome.

I have busy personal life with two children and two dogs, in my spare time I like to get away from the city and be in the countryside around nature.

The opportunity to write about ADHD and being a Social Worker sparked my interest in creative writing, 'Spinning the Plates' is my first poem. The poem is my experience of managing life and career pre-diagnosis, always feeling like I was one step behind. I was always conscious that people saw my potential, but I could never achieve it. Since being diagnosed, I have spoken to colleagues about it, some of whom have confided that they have ADHD themselves but had been worried to disclose it.

I hope that the poem provides other people some affirmation of their experiences.

Shout out - My two wonderful children, Cayden and Willow and my Dad who has always believed in me.

- Mark Stockley-Haylock

I'm Mark, a 40 year old student social worker, currently in the adult learning disabilities team at Darlington Borough Council, and I absolutely love it. I have lived in Durham all my life, I wouldn't change it for the world. I enjoy a wide variety of pastimes; walking the dogs (especially at the Lake District), playing golf, watching Newcastle United, and of course playing PC games.

Shout out - I wish to thank my Wife; Leigh-Anne, without her god knows where I would be! My daughter Sophie for keeping my on the straight and narrow. My mum for being the best mum anyone could ask for! And finally, but by no means least... Andy, my brother, my friend and my confidant, if you read this, you already know how much your friendship means to me.

Twitter: @NUFC_GolfDad

- Maximillian Hawker

Maximilian Hawker is a children's social worker and writer who lives in Croydon, South London, with his wife and two daughters. He is author of the novels Breaking the Foals and Rory Hobble and the Voyage to Haligogen (both published by Unbound). Since childhood, he has suffered with severe obsessive compulsive disorder (OCD) and does media advocacy on behalf of the charity OCD Action as and when he can.

@MaxHawker

linkedin.com/in/maximilian-hawker-8a5a2714b/

- *Natalie Woodd*

I'm originally from Gosport, Hampshire in 1971, where my wonderful mum still lives. Since 1994, I've called the west country home. It has been a privilege to co-parent my daughter, Charlotte, and watch her grow from a loving and sensitive child into an independent woman who knows her own mind. Fate, and her dad, also brought my incredible stepdaughter, Pippa, who navigates the world without fear. I also have two very badly behaved dogs who make me laugh every day.

In 2019, 32 years after leaving school, I joined City College, Plymouth. They enabled me to achieve, with the support of my peers and lecturers, an Access to Higher Education Diploma (Health and Social Care), update my English and gain that elusive Math's qualification within a 12 month period. I loved the smaller class sizes and thrived during discussions; I could articulate well but struggled to write my thoughts. Although my grades were good, I became aware that I had to work harder and for longer than my peers.

The following year, 2020. I joined the University of Plymouth and am currently in my final year and out on placement with a local authority fostering team, which has been a privilege. After a year of home study during the pandemic, it was in year two when I noticed other people's coping strategies that mirrored my own. I was finally tested for and diagnosed with Dyslexia aged 51!

It's not the same for everyone, but my creative thinking suddenly made sense. Dyslexia enabled me to present information differently, but I also felt cheated that I'd spent a lifetime having to navigate life, work, and education without it being picked up by professionals. Many lecturers' skills enabled them to navigate seamlessly adapting their teaching styles. However, I do think it's an area of huge learning opportunity within the education management system. Clunky marking systems can disproportionately impact neurodivergent students; their self-esteem, their ability to work, and their results. The research is there.

I have gained so much from many of the staff and those in my cohort who have been a huge part of my learning journey. As someone who learns in practice, I have learned to utilise extra training resources, which have added depth to my understanding. I would encourage everyone, but especially those who are ND to embrace podcasts, webinars, seminars, and training days as they have been hugely helpful to my own learning.

Shout out - Dr Judith Rowbotham to whom I'll always be grateful. She has been a mentor and friend who has helped me navigate academic writing and module briefs, prior to and since my diagnosis.

Siobhan and the entire team at Student Social Work Connect were a huge part of my journey and helped me to untangle theory and models in a relatable way when the books didn't make sense.

My cohort pals who made being part of the 'Covid Cohort' bearable – you know who you are!

Jen Downham – from that very first day when we bonded over being late to being 'attacked' by moorland ponies trying to get into the car with us... and beyond!

Beth Moran, Sue Cook and Julia Wheeler from the University of Plymouth – thank you for the guidance, support and patience.

Twitter: @socialworkplan
Instagram: @socialworkplan
Linkedin: Natalie Woodd

- *Nathan Pierson*

My name is Nathan Pierson, i have autism and verbal dyspraxia and i lived in the beautiful Mournes. I am well known landscape and nature photographer based in Northern Ireland, i travelling all around Northern Ireland, Ireland and other countries to doing my photography. I really enjoyed any minute of it, i always seeing everything through my eyes that no else can see with my autism and i am so proud of doing photography. All of my photos are available to purchase from myself, my studio and workshop, local craft fairs and some local outlets too. To follow my amazing photography journey, please visit Nat Photography Northern Ireland on Facebook and Instagram and give my social media pages a wee follow. Thank you so much for supporting my photography work, following Nat Photography Northern Ireland on Facebook and Instagram and being a massive part of my photography journey

I also won UTV Pride of Britain Northern Ireland Regional Fundraiser of the year along with 2 other awards for my fundraising work which i raised over £60,000 for local charities since 2015. I love doing fundraising too. I meet lots of celebrities while attending Pride of Britain Awards Gala in London and i really enjoyed any minute of it.

Shout out - I would like to say a personal thank you to Siobhan and Kelly for including some of my photos in their new book and also I would like to say a massive thank you to my mum & dad, all of my family & friends, Donard School Banbridge and all of my supporters and followers who always supporting me and being a massive part on my photography, fundraising and autism journey.

- Nicola Jordan

Nicola Jordan is a social work practice master's student, on the Think Ahead program.

Prior to commencing her masters, Nicola spent time in America, where she wrote and illustrated a book to be used in occupational therapy sessions with children, to help them understand the Corona virus.

Nicola also helped to organise and run a fundraiser in aid of the ACLU, raising over $10,000 during the Black Lives Matter protests.

Nicola is also an art lover and has sold her paintings to independent art shops in the states.

Nicola holds a degree in counselling, coaching, and mentoring, and a post graduate degree in teaching.

She believes that kindness and compassion can change the world and strives to promote these values in her practice.

Upon completion of her master's degree, Nicola intends to study further and would like to inform best practice when working with neurodivergence.

Shout out - My son, Felix. The source of all my joy and inspiration.

Twitter: @Nikojord
Linkedin: nicolamjordan

- Pete Nevison

I have had a young life of difficulty both educationally, emotionally, and with regards to stability. I have grown and learned over my career and also built my resilience. I continue to do this. I have my fantastic support networks to thank for some of my ability to do this. Some of my biography is really in the story because it all forms part of my journey, I have been Dyslexic my whole life. It is my approach and view towards it that has changed.

Shout out - I would like to thank my wife for supporting me to pursue a new dream, returning to education to build my future. She was not my wife when I started this journey, she could have run but she didn't.

Social media - Peter Nevison on linkedin. My other social media accounts are about making homebrew beer, that isn't the right chat.

- Rachael Duke

Rachael Duke is a Social Worker, who qualified at age 34 with a first-class degree from Buckinghamshire New University in 2021. She has since worked in Adult Social Care, as part of a newly formed transition team, within Oxfordshire County Council. Rachael aspires to become a Practice Educator in the future, where she hopes to support students progressing into the world of Social Work.

Prior to Social Work, Rachael had a career in the Royal Air Force. She was also a Foster Carer, along with her husband and is Mum to two children.

Shout out - I wish to give acknowledgement to all my Social Work and Coordinator colleagues within the Moving into Adulthood Team at Oxfordshire County Council. Giving special thanks for their ongoing guidance, encouragement, and support.

My husband Kieron and children, Finley and Adelaide.

- *Rose Matthews*

I am an older white person (aged 63), and identify as female, leaning towards non-binary. I'm a former social worker and academic (I was Rose Barton then) and I'm proud to be socialist and woke. I have just experienced a late in life epiphany - if you had asked me who I was five years ago I would hardly have had a clue.

From the moment I learned to speak, read, and write I loved the subtlety and precision of language: its definitions, dialects and sounds, and the way words looked on the page. I made sense of the world and the people in it through fiction and non-fiction. The books I read as a child were my 'social stories'. As a young teenager my mother helped me to solve the problem of how I might earn a living one day by buying me a series of career stories, with titles like 'Anne Becomes a Secretary'. When I read 'Frances Becomes an Almoner' I was hooked. I could imagine how desperately difficult it would be to be stuck in hospital longing to be at home. Frances could make this happen.

I started volunteering in long stay hospitals and made deep connections with people who were marginalised, discriminated against and de-humanised, without fully understanding why I had so much empathy with them. I was set on becoming a social worker and eventually found my way into the profession through a somewhat circuitous route.

My career was adventurous and unconventional – I was passionately engaged in every role, but my personal relationships suffered due to overwork. It was not obvious back then how much sensory and social environments affected me. I had repeated burnouts after which I would recover just enough to force myself to carry on. It was relentless and gruelling. Although I found great fulfilment in my work, I was constantly exhausted and on the point of overwhelm.

For many years my struggles were well-hidden by a thin veneer of coping, with tumultuous anguish underneath. I searched for answers and couldn't find any. The only common denominator in all these situations was me, but none of the theories I came up with made any sense. By the time I reached my late 50s I was traumatised by the past and scared of the future; I had a burning desire to work out what was going on so I could enter old age less fearfully.

I was almost 59 when I discovered that I was autistic. By then I'd graduated with bachelor's and master's degrees, qualified and practised as a social worker, been a social work academic and educator, and spent years in criminal justice, learning and development, and social care roles. I'd been married twice and had two children. Gaining this clarity was life-changing. I had answers to all the questions I'd ever asked about myself. Reframing my past assuaged feelings of guilt, shame and failure I had long been haunted by.

Finding out that I am autistic has given me a renewed sense of belonging and purpose. I am an insider in autistic spaces, not a hanger-on on the margins of mainstream society. I have become a researcher and activist in the fight for autistic freedom and rights. The upsurgence in autistic self-advocacy is shifting the balance of power. Equality and inclusion lie ahead.

Shout out - I would like to pay tribute to my mother, Jane Ellam, who devoted over sixty years to voluntary social care work. She made a huge difference to many people's lives and inspired my interest in social work.

@NortherlyRose
@Autism_R_and_D
@SensoryJoy

- Sam Keeton

I am a Social Worker, working as a Team Manager in the Adults with Learning Disabilities Team in Bradford Council. I am a Practice Educator and Best Interest Assessor and really love helping the next generation.

I am a mother of 2 wonderful ND kids Willow and Xander. I am Vegan and passionate about Nature and the Planet (Born@346ppm). My children attend a Steiner School as I feel this is such a wonderful way for our children to learn in harmony with Nature as a pace that they need.

I am a big nerd and love Warhammer, D&D, Video games (I have a retro console collection) and anything fantasy and Sci-fi.

I am very passionate about Empowerment, Inclusion, Equality, Rights and LOVE ♥!

I feel all people, no matter which circumstances you were born into, should be loved and be given the opportunity to be included and heard equal to everyone around them.

My favorite saying: "Be the change you want to see in the world".

Shout out - How much space do I have? Lol.

Firstly, shout out to my Mother for doing her best to raise a non-stop talkative ND daughter, whilst working and caring for her ND and MH husband and my awesome older sister.

To my husband Ben (can't be an easy job being married to me) and my wonderful Kids Willow and Xander.

To ALL the amazing people I started my career with at Calderdale:

Those who came to Bradford, Rob Mitchell, Elaine James, Kirsty McLeod, Ian Burgess and Jack Skinner, and those who didn't Andrea Richards, Tina Brayshaw and Mark Barber.

You all showed me in different ways how to be the best kind of social worker, I owe a lot to you all.

And finally to my AMAZING Team who put up with my oddities and put their heart and soul into what they do. I'm so proud of you all! ♥

Twitter: @Samjkeeton
@LDteambradford

- Sandy Symonds

I qualified as a Social Worker in 2004. I gained a Master of Arts in Advanced Social Work in 2019. I am a Practice Educator and enjoy supporting students on their placements. I am also a trained coach. Much of my practice has been in statutory Childrens Social Care, primarily working within children and family settings. More recently I have moved into leadership and developmental roles. I have been fortunate to be part of some great teams developing and delivering innovative practice. I am particularly interested in developing a coaching culture within Social Work practice.

Twitter: @sandy_symo

- Sheila AM Leighton

I sat and wrote this piece, inspired by my struggle and encouraged by those who could see my potential and the need to embrace who I am.

Who am I? Many have asked this question, and there are many labels I can attach myself. I am someone's child, sister, wife, mother, grandmother, friend, and colleague, but I don't fit into a box! While I am many things to many people, this does not mean I am a Chameleon; I am authentic to who I am. There are just different sides to me, depending on who you are. My profession as a social worker fits my personality. I am sociable, approachable, inquisitive, empathetic, intuitive, a problem solver, and so much more, all wrapped in this person called Sheila mostly and Anne-Marie sometimes, who strives for social justice and an equal platform for all.

My Queen, one of the most accepting and loving people I am blessed to know and who is my mum, encouraged us all to be the best we could be. I was the quietest of her five children, and within that quiet space of peace and harmony, I developed an understanding of myself and the people around me. I studied people from a noticeably early age and how they interacted with each other, which fascinates me to this day. I came to understand that I see the world differently. I felt embarrassed and thought I was not whole or complete in some way, trying to fit in with my very academic siblings. I was not aware of my neurodiversity, not understanding my unique and creative way of thinking and pulling things together to make sense in my world.

I grew up in East London and was educated there but went to Middlesex University, where I gained my Social Work degree – based on assignments, not examinations. Many years later, I returned to the University of East London to do my Doctorate in social work and was fully diagnosed in June 2021 with Dyslexia and other traits, which are me ☺. With this knowledge, I found an acceptance of myself. Now in 2023, I am in the final stage of my studies, and it is nearing its end.

Without key people along my journey who encouraged and pushed me to show my ability to engage and develop within the gaps I could see, I would have continued to hide in the shadows and doubt my abilities, not celebrating my achievements.

My way of thinking is not a hindrance or a flaw in my matrix. I still battle with that imposter syndrome from time to time, especially in new environments. However, I now define who I am.

I hope you enjoy the read.

Shout out - I thank God for every step I have made and for carrying me when I didn't even know I needed to be carried!

My reason for waking in the morning is my mum, Ron, my husband, the three J's in my life (two sons and daughter-in-law), My grandbabies ☺ My three siblings who give me enough jokes, Aunty J, who heard the poem and gave the title.

Amma Anane-Agyei for encouraging me to truly understand the world as a Black person taking me to and through doors that I would never have gone through.

Dr Jo Finch for supporting me throughout my struggle for acceptance.

- *Siobhan Maclean*

I have been a social worker for 33 years and I have been a mum for almost the same length of time. I have two amazing daughters who have put up with me "spoiling everything with social work theory" when I talk about theory in relation to everything!

I have recently moved to Northern Ireland, and I feel like I have eventually "found my home." I love welcoming social workers to retreat here to reflect and am learning new things from those workers every day.

Shout out - to my two wonderful daughters, Fliss and Rosie who are making the world a better place.

www.siobhanmaclean.co.uk

@siobhanmaclean

- Vicky Butterfield

Vicky was born in Bradford and qualified as a social worker when she was twenty seven. In the ten years since qualifying she has worked in Statutory Children's Services in both child protection teams and as a supervising social worker in fostering. Vicky moved to CAMHS in 2020, currently working in the neurodevelopmental team and has recently completed a postgraduate certificate in Systemic Practice (Family Therapy). It was with the support of her team that she realised the need to have an ADHD assessment and was diagnosed in 2022.

Vicky and her husband Jonathan are proud foster parents to a wonderful young lady, Zoe. When not working Vicky likes to travel, walk her Saluki, and train for triathlons but alas does not own a gecko (yet).

Shout out - To my mum Julie, sister Sam, nephew Daniel, Grandma Wendy and Grandad John, best friend Jono and, last but not least, my wonderful husband Jonathan, thank you all for loving me and my quirky ways.

Instagram: @theuntrainedathlete

- Yulin Cheng

Yulin Cheng is an autistic self-advocate with a degree in Law and Politics. Born in Singapore, she now resides in Hong Kong where she is doing her PhD study in social work. Her research employs a critical lens and mix-methods design to look at the impact of the social environment on the well-being of autistic adults. She shares a flat with Happy the cat (pictured).

Shout out - I would like to thank the people who have supported and encouraged me during these difficult times, my autistic comrades and neurodiversity allies, with special thanks to Teresa Girolamo, Rebecca Jackson, Kathy Leadbitter, Sonia Soans, for their advice, friendship and mentorship. I would also like to thank my project collaborators for putting up with my lack of efficiency and for their kindness. Thank you also to friends outside my research and advocacy circle and the baristas in my local cafés where I spent hours working in. Thank you to the publisher for your interest in my story, I honestly did not think I am going to make it for submission but your generosity and belief in me made all the difference.

Twitter: Yu_Lin_Cheng